Sublime Vegetarian

To Elva,

Have fun in
the Kitchen

Bill Jones

Sublime

Vegetarian

Bill Jones

Douglas & McIntyre
Vancouver/Toronto

Douglas & McIntyre Ltd.
2323 Quebec Street, Suite 201
Vancouver, British Columbia V5T 4S7

CANADIAN CATALOGUING IN PUBLICATION DATA

Jones, W.A. (William Allen), 1959–
The sublime vegetarian
Includes index.

ISBN 1-55054-741-0

1. Vegatarian cookery. I. Title.
TX837.J66 1999   641.5'636   C99-910666-X

Editing by Saeko Usukawa and Lucy Kenward
Design by cardigan.com
Photography by John Sherlock
Photography assistant: Alastair Bird
Propping by Joanne Strongman

Printed and bound in Canada by Friesens
Printed on acid-free paper

Canadä

The publisher gratefully
acknowledges the support of the Canada
Council for the Arts and of the British Columbia
Ministry of Tourism, Small Business and Culture. The
publisher also acknowledges the financial support of
the Government of Canada through the Book
Publishing Industry Development
Program.

Foreword by Sinclair Philip *ix*

Introduction *xi*

Acknowledgements *xii*

Vegetable Cooking Techniques *1*

Pantry Basics

    Homemade Stocks and Sauces *5*

    Bottled Sauces, Oils and Vinegars *17*

    Herbs for Flavouring *21*

    Wine and Vegetarian Cuisine *23*

Appetizers *25*

Vegetarian Sushi *33*

Soups and Chowders *43*

Noodle Soups *55*

Green Salads *67*

Vegetable Salads *79*

Tapas and Flatbreads *91*

Noodles and Pasta *103*

Rice *115*

Beans and Tofu *125*

Potatoes *133*

Desserts *145*

Index *156*

＊

This book is
for farmers, gardeners
and all stewards of the land.
It is also a tribute to Evelyn
Wilkinson, a lover of
gardens and
books.

Foreword

by Sinclair Philip, Sooke Harbour House

It is delightful to be able to pen the foreword for a book written by such a widely travelled and accomplished chef and cookbook author as Bill Jones. I have known Bill both as a chef at Sooke Harbour House and in his capacity as a community food activist and intellectual. For years, between his jaunts around the world, Bill and I have supported the regional, seasonal and organic approach to cooking within several organizations. We have also shared a passion for wild foraged foods, and Bill has gone on to become a recognized authority on regional mushrooms. How could I turn down an invitation to write a foreword for someone who looks upon humans as "merely an advanced form of truffle-hunting pigs"?

Bill's cooking has always emphasized regional, seasonal ingredients – sometimes with a little of the Asian flair that has influenced all of us here on the West Coast. Regional, seasonal, organic cuisine has been the predominant approach to food in most parts of the world throughout the centuries. It is a cooking style rooted in the plants, animals, "terroir" (soil, climate and topography), history, and peoples of an area. This is the approach that has produced the world's great cuisines and best dishes.

At Sooke Harbour House, our menu changes radically from one season to the next, depending upon what local foragers and farmers can provide. To us, it means that produce comes to the kitchen in the full bloom of its flavours and aromas. Local produce is sweeter and more satisfying than the tempting, widely travelled asparagus or tomatoes that appear on the grocer's shelves while snow is still on the ground. The chefs in our kitchens here have developed an increased familiarity with local producers and their products. The direct relationships with and understanding of suppliers has resulted in much better quality and a wider variety of products. Consequently, we respect the products to a greater degree and learn how to use them to obtain greater gustatory rewards.

Why is it important that good chefs and home cooks use regional produce? Because regional produce adds much more variety, flavour and nutrition to the dinner table. There are literally hundreds of local ingredients in most parts of North America that are rarely ever consumed in people's homes within their own region, and these are often the best, or most intriguing, ingredients available. In addition, local produce can be obtained at the peak of sweetness, flavour and ripeness due to short delivery times. Quick delivery times also help avoid nutrient loss since, as produce ages, it oxidizes, resulting in a deterioration in flavour and nutritional value.

Regional goes hand in hand with seasonal. Seasonal foods have been the primary foods consumed just about everywhere in the world until very recently. Everything tastes best in its season. Seasonal, local ingredients are the foundation of all great cuisines. Many of the world's best chefs do not pretend that strawberries and melons know no winter. Why give up the sensory reward of nature's seasonal offerings for pale, insipid, facsimiles? In the winter, locally grown kale or leeks, properly cooked, really will taste better than corn trucked or flown in from the four corners of the earth.

No discussion of modern food would be complete without some reference to organic agriculture. The use of organic food, whenever possible, has always been important to Bill and myself. It is in everyone's interest to eat organic produce since the quality and sustainability of our food supply is increasingly at risk, due to the overexploitation of our agricultural and aquatic resources for quick economic returns. Anyone with a

social conscience must consider the fact
that organic methods are driven by an ethical determination to sustain the soil and sur-
rounding lands and to reduce our ecological
footprint. Vegetarianism, or diets that rely
heavily on vegetables and fruit and organic
production, help to conserve natural
resources, solve rather than create environ-
mental problems, and help to reduce the
pollution of our air, water, soil and food.

Organic and small-scale agriculture is
booming here in the Pacific Northwest and
across Canada, but its fragile beginnings
require our continued support. Unique
foods are emerging as an important component of regional cuisines, and the revival of
some forms of polyculture provides us with
far more foods of high quality than was the
case twenty years ago.

Over the past few years, we have witnessed the arrival of a new generation of
specialty and organic food producers in
many parts of North America. For instance,
on Vancouver Island where I live, we can
find white spring asparagus, a wide range of
exciting organic vegetables, a year-round
supply of dozens of different fresh organic
herbs, wildflower honey, delicious organic
beans and grains, and glorious salad greens –
not to mention the remarkable seasonal
selection of heritage tomatoes, organic
garlics and wonderful tree fruits from other
parts of our region.

Since 1979, the culinary team at Sooke
Harbour House has strived to cook as much
as possible with the best local, seasonal and
organic ingredients. Most of our victualizing,
from sweet cicely root to salal berries, from
pine mushrooms to Coast Salish nodding
onion, emanates from our own organic gardens, or from nearby Vancouver Island farms
and mountain forests, even vegetables from
the sea. We have successfully nurtured our
own organic gardens to the point where they
provide a considerable amount of the inn's
vegetables, fruits, edible flowers and herbs.
We have also supported local farmers and
foragers, many of whom have now become
important suppliers to the entire region.
Small-scale, organic, varied regional agriculture is now a reality in southern Vancouver
Island. At the inn, our menus change daily to
accommodate the agricultural treasures
brought to our door. This is food that helps
restore body and soul for all of us. We have
always believed that the best and tastiest
foods are found near their source. Through
experience, we have also found that what
grows together, goes together.

Introduction

Perched on the edge of the Pacific rim, the west coast of North America is an exciting place to explore vegetarian cooking. It is a place where a contemporary cooking style has evolved, influenced by the strong presence of Asian cultures and the bounty of nature. The same temperate climate that grows gigantic cedars and Douglas firs nurtures the cultivation of an impressive range of produce. The food we eat is shaped by our position on the edge of a continent, on the edge of diverse cultures and on the edge of a new awareness of the positive power of food.

For centuries, since the First Nations peoples began living on the west coast, the inhabitants have celebrated and thrived on the fertile cycle of the seasons. Modern life and the emergence of global sources of food have confused and erased many of our connections to the seasons. But it wasn't that long ago that our grandparents used to preserve seasonal harvests by means of frequent canning sessions and careful storage in cool root cellars. Today, the convenience of the supermarket and the constant influence of the advertising world have led us away from the simple, whole foods of our ancestors, towards increasingly processed and engineered foods. Luckily, this ominous trend has given rise to a positive counter-trend. As we discover more about the human body, our awareness of the part food plays increases and reveals the strong influence that diet has on our physical and mental well-being.

Food is more important than just a fuel for our bodies. Food also plays a central part in our family and cultural lives. Food accompanies our celebrations and helps to form a bond with those we share it with. As patterns of immigration change, we have witnessed once exotic cuisines like Thai, Vietnamese, Malaysian and South Asian becoming available in the smallest of neighbourhoods and towns. These cuisines, with their emphasis on rice, beans and grains, have helped prove that good vegetarian food can be tasty and simple to prepare – in addition to balancing our diets. Vegetarianism is becoming a valid option for many people for a host of economic, health and ethical reasons.

As our small village expands into a global community, we can use food as a stepping stone to understanding, respecting and appreciating our neighbours. The exchange of foods is a process that has been going on for many centuries. The Americas exported chocolate, corn, potatoes and chili peppers to the world. In return, we received the gifts of garlic, ginger, soybeans and rice. The future will bring about even more fusion of cooking as we experience and embrace the diverse cultures of the planet. Influences from Argentina to Alaska will be fused into the giant melting pot of our diet and inspire recipes adapted to our modern needs.

– Bill Jones

Acknowledgements

A special thank you to Scott McIntyre, Saeko Usukawa, Terri Wershler, Kelly Mitchell and all the team at Douglas & McIntyre. It was also very enjoyable to work with food photographer extraordinaire John Sherlock and his extended family, and to play in his studio for a few days.

I'm especially grateful to Sinclair and Fredrica Philip. Sooke Harbour House, their magical country inn, was a fascinating place at which to learn and an unforgettable place to live.

A big hug and thank you to my favourite gardener, Lynn, my wife and supplier of fresh herbs. By the way, the cat is asking that you plant more catnip.

And I am beholden to my family, particularly my parents, Joan and Bill, for teaching me to eat my vegetables and to enjoy the pleasures of the garden.

Vegetable Cooking Techniques

To extract the maximum flavour and nutrients from vegetables, you must use the correct cooking technique. In most cases, do not overcook them. Lightly cooking vegetables retains vitamins and can neutralize some unpleasant-tasting enzymes and proteins. Cooking vegetables properly also adds to the pleasurable texture and often aids the digestive process.

Sautéing or Stir-Frying

Sautéing or stir-frying involves tossing and quick cooking over high heat. Oil is used to brown and bring out a great deal of flavour. Place a dry stainless steel or cast-iron pan over high heat for 2 to 3 minutes. This expands the pores of metal pans, allowing the oil to penetrate and to keep items from sticking during cooking. Add the oil, swirling to coat the bottom of the pan. (NOTE: Do not place a dry nonstick skillet over high heat, as that can damage the coating and cause the pan to warp; add the oil right after you place the pan on the heat.) Heat until the oil is just smoking, then add the ingredients, stirring quickly with a wooden spatula or spoon to coat them evenly with the hot oil and seasonings. Cook the vegetables over high heat (or medium-high) until they are brightly coloured and beginning to soften.

Pan-Frying

Pan-frying involves cooking items in oil over high heat to caramelize them or to produce a light crust. Place a dry stainless steel or cast-iron pan over high heat for 2 to 3 minutes, then add the oil and heat for 2 to 3 minutes. (NOTE: If you are using a nonstick skillet, add the oil as soon as you place the pan on the heat.) Add the ingredients, then reduce the heat to medium-high. Shake the pan to distribute the oil under the items and to allow even browning. Cook until golden brown on both sides. To get rid of excess fat, temporarily remove the items from the pan and drain the oil onto a plate lined with a paper towel.

Blanching

Blanching helps to partially cook and tenderize vegetables. Bring a large, heavy pot of water to a boil. Salt the water generously (the salt helps to set the colour of most vegetables, particularly green ones), then add the vegetables. Return to the boil and cook vegetables for 5 to 7 minutes, or until tender and brightly coloured. Drain the vegetables in a colander (or use a slotted spoon to lift them out if you wish to reuse the water). Place the vegetables in a bowl filled with cold water and ice cubes, to stop them from continuing to cook. When the vegetables are cool, remove them from the water and drain. The cooked vegetables may be chilled in the refrigerator for 1 or 2 hours before using.

Roasting

Roasting vegetables caramelizes the natural sugars present in them to bring out a wonderful flavour. Use a heavy roasting pan and preheat the oven, usually to 350°F (180°C). Place the dry roasting pan in the oven and preheat it for 5 minutes. In a bowl, combine the vegetables with the oil and seasonings, tossing well to coat. Transfer vegetables to the hot pan and roast in the oven for 10 to 15 minutes. Remove from the oven and stir the vegetables to ensure even browning. Return to the oven for another 10 to 15 minutes, or until the vegetables are tender and browned. Note that onions and yams have high sugar levels, so they brown very quickly.

Steaming

Steaming is a healthy way to cook vegetables, as this method uses little or no oil. The vegetables tend to retain more flavour and nutrients than with any other cooking method. The best tool for steaming is a stacking metal steamer (sold in Asian markets): it has a bottom pot, with stacking trays for layers of steaming, and a domed lid for the top. Pour 1 cup (250 ml) of water into the bottom pot. You can place aromatics such as ginger, garlic, lemon grass or kaffir lime in the water to infuse the vegetables with extra flavour. Place the vegetables that take longest to cook on the lowest layer, with delicate ones (like broccoli and asparagus) on higher layers. Cover the top layer with the lid, bring the water to a boil over high heat and steam the vegetables for about 7 to 8 minutes, or until they are just tender.

A wok or large pot can easily be converted to a steamer. Pour 2 cups (500 ml) of water into the wok or pot, and place a heatproof bowl upside-down in the bottom of it. Arrange the vegetables on a heatproof plate and place the plate on the bowl. Cover the wok or pot with a large lid (or round baking tray). Bring the water to a boil over high heat and steam the vegetables.

Grilling

Grilling increases the flavour of vegetables without using a lot of oil. Bitter-tasting vegetables like radicchio and endive are literally transformed when tossed in olive oil and garlic, then lightly charred on the grill. Grilling over wood or charcoal produces the most flavour, but a gas grill is more convenient. Stovetop cast-iron grills make nice-looking marks on vegetables but do little to help the flavour.

First, preheat the grill. Place the vegetables in a bowl and drizzle with a little oil; season with salt and pepper, then toss well. Transfer the vegetables to the hot grill and cook on each side until they are tender and beginning to char. The cooking time will vary with the type and thickness of the vegetables. Most vegetables are ready when easily pierced with a fork.

Pantry Basics

Homemade Stocks and Sauces

A well-supplied pantry gives you the ability to create delicious dishes at a moment's notice. Some of the pantry basics are real time-savers, while others add flavour and dash to the food. Many of the pantry items that you can make will keep well for months.

Stocks and cooking liquids are used to gently cook vegetables, to release and absorb flavour from sautéed vegetables, spices and herbs, and to meld all the flavours together in a harmonious blend. They also form the base for flavourful sauces and soups. Clear stocks are made by slowly simmering raw vegetables and flavourings. Brown stocks are made by first roasting or sautéing vegetables and aromatics in oil until browned, then simmering them gently in water until all the flavours are released. The colour and flavour can be enhanced by adding soy sauce to the final product.

Almost any vegetable can be used to make a flavourful stock, but place only fresh vegetable trimmings in a stockpot. Leeks add richness to the broth, carrots add sweetness, mushrooms add body, and celery adds balance and salt. Strongly flavoured vegetables such as fennel, celery, parsnips, asparagus and Brussels sprouts can overpower a stock, so use them in moderation. Avoid using eggplant, as it adds an unpleasant bitterness. A little charring, especially with onions, adds a pleasant flavour and colour to the stock, but heavily charred vegetables will contribute a strong burnt flavour and should be removed before the water is added.

Hot stock should be cooled to room temperature before storing, as placing hot stock in the refrigerator keeps the liquid at a critical temperature for bacterial production. Cool quickly on a wire rack, with the lid off the pot. Transfer the stock to small containers or plastic zip-lock bags, leaving at least 1 inch (2 cm) headroom at the top for expansion when the stock is frozen. Label each container with the name and date of the stock. Use within 1 month for best results.

Flavoured liquids often may be used instead of stock. Apple juice or cider is a handy substitute for stock in many dishes, as its natural pectin coats the mouth and allows flavours to linger on the palate. If the natural sweetness is unsuitable for the dish, you can balance it with a squeeze of fresh lemon juice near the end of cooking.

A host of new dehydrated vegetable products are available, and flavourful substitutes for stock can be obtained by soaking dried vegetables, reconstituting freeze-dried vegetable stocks or using cubes of concentrated vegetable stock. Look for products that are free of monosodium glutamate (MSG) and low in sodium. Health food stores are the best source for these specialty products.

Roasted Vegetable Stock

Makes 4 quarts (4 L)
Oven at 350°F (180°C)

2 cups	large onions, sliced	500 mL
2 cups	carrots, sliced	500 mL
2 cups	celery ribs, sliced	500 mL
1 head	garlic, cut in half	1 head
2 Tb	olive oil	30 mL
	Salt and pepper to taste	
2 Tb	tomato paste	30 mL
4 quarts	water	4 L
3	bay leaves	3
2 Tb	rosemary, chopped	30 mL
2 Tb	sage, chopped	30 mL
10	black peppercorns	10

1 In a roasting pan, combine onions, carrots, celery and garlic. Add olive oil and season with salt and pepper, tossing well to coat. Roast in the oven for 30 minutes, or until vegetables are soft and browned. Add tomato paste and mix in well. Return to the oven and roast for an additional 15 minutes.

2 Remove from the oven and transfer the vegetables to a large stockpot. Pour a little boiling water into the roasting pan to deglaze and pour into the stockpot. Add water, bay leaves, rosemary, sage and peppercorns. Stir well. Over high heat, bring the mixture to a boil. Reduce the heat and simmer uncovered for 1 hour.

3 Strain the stock into a clean pot and discard the vegetables. Place the pot on a wire rack. Cool to room temperature, then refrigerate overnight and freeze. Will keep frozen for 1 month.

A good homemade vegetable stock adds life to any soup or sauce you make. Roasting the vegetables produces a stock with a rich flavour and an appealing, deep brown colour. Try adding other vegetables like parsnips, mushrooms, fennel and peppers.

Fragrant Vegetable Stock

Makes 4 quarts (4 L)

4 quarts	water	4 L
2 cups	onions, sliced	500 mL
2 cups	leeks, sliced	500 mL
1 cup	celery ribs, sliced	250 mL
1 cup	fennel bulbs, sliced	250 mL
3	bay leaves	3
5	black peppercorns	5
1 head	garlic, cut in half	1 head
2 Tb	coriander seeds	30 mL
1 tsp	salt	5 mL

1 In a large stockpot, combine all the ingredients. Bring the mixture to a boil, then reduce the heat and simmer uncovered for 1 hour.

2 Strain the stock into a clean pot and discard the vegetables. Place the pot on a wire rack. Cool to room temperature, then refrigerate overnight and freeze. Will keep frozen for 1 month.

Almost any aromatic vegetable can be added to this nutritious broth – try carrots, mushrooms, cauliflower and shallots. Poaching vegetables over gentle heat brings out the best flavours and produces a clear, fragrant stock. For a more robust flavour and a golden colour, brown the onions first in a bit of olive oil. Another variation is to roast the fennel and garlic first.

Fresh Mushroom Stock

Makes 4 quarts (4 L)

4 quarts	water	4 L
1 lb	mushrooms, sliced (button, portobello, shiitake or oyster)	500 g
2 cups	large onions, sliced	500 mL
1 cup	celery ribs, sliced	250 mL
1 head	garlic, cut in half	1 head
1 Tb	rosemary, chopped	15 mL
1 cup	white wine (optional)	250 mL

1 In a large stockpot, combine all the ingredients. Bring to a boil, then reduce the heat and simmer uncovered for 1 hour.

2 Strain the stock into a clean pot and discard the mushrooms and vegetables. Place the pot on a wire rack. Cool to room temperature, then refrigerate overnight and freeze. Will keep frozen for 1 month.

Mushrooms have played a part in Chinese traditional medicine for thousands of years. Recent scientific studies have indicated substantial health-giving properties exist in many types of fungi. They are reputed to boost overall energy and immunity levels, lower cholesterol and may help to cure the common cold.

The shiitake is my favourite mushroom for this stock. Use them whole and remove after cooking to enjoy as tender braised mushrooms.

Dried Mushroom Stock

Makes 4 quarts (4 L)

4 quarts	water	4 L
¼ cup	dried mushrooms (8–10 pieces)	50 mL
2 cups	large onions, sliced	500 mL
1 head	whole garlic, cut in half	1 head
2 slices	ginger	2 slices
1 Tb	sweet soy sauce (p 18)	15 mL
1 tsp	hot sauce (or to taste)	5 mL

1 In a large stockpot, combine all the ingredients. Bring to a boil, then reduce the heat and simmer uncovered for 1 hour.

2 Strain the stock into a clean pot and discard the vegetables. Place on a wire rack. Cool to room temperature, then refrigerate overnight and freeze. Will keep frozen for 1 month.

Many kinds of mushrooms are available dried: shiitake, oyster, porcini, morel, black trumpet, wood ear and pine. You can use dried mushroom slices or grind them into mushroom powder. Before grinding, make sure the dried mushrooms are brittle (toast in an oven or in a dry pan for 2 to 3 minutes). If you do not have a spice mill to grind the dried mushrooms, use a small coffee grinder after cleaning it thoroughly. Grind until a fine powder is formed. The powder is a simple way to instantly boost the flavour of any stock, sauce or soup.

The sweet soy sauce adds a wonderful body to the stock. Another type of soy sauce may be used instead – or it may be omitted altogether.

❖◆❖◆❖◆❖◆❖◆❖◆❖◆❖◆❖◆❖◆❖◆❖◆❖◆❖◆❖

Tomato Sauce

Makes 3 quarts (3 L)

2 Tb	olive oil	30 mL
2 cups	onions, minced	500 mL
3 Tb	garlic, minced	45 mL
1 cup	celery, sliced	250 mL
½ lb	mushrooms, diced	250 g
1	zucchini, seeded and diced	1
8 cups	canned stewed tomatoes and liquid	2 L
2	bay leaves	2
1 Tb	each marjoram, basil, thyme, rosemary	15 mL
1 Tb	honey	15 mL
	Hot sauce to taste (optional)	
	Salt and pepper to taste	

1 In a stockpot, heat olive oil. Add onions and garlic. Sauté over medium-high heat for 5 minutes, or until onions begin to brown. Add celery, mushrooms and zucchini, then sauté for 2 to 3 minutes. Add tomatoes, bay leaves, herbs, honey, hot sauce, salt and pepper. Bring to a boil, then reduce the heat and simmer uncovered for 1 hour, stirring occasionally.

2 Pour the sauce into a clean pot and place on a wire rack. Cool to room temperature, then refrigerate overnight. Will keep refrigerated for 2 to 3 days and frozen for 1 month.

Tomato *sauce is one of the foundations of good cooking. Combined with pasta, it is the epitome of fast food – dinner can be on the table in 15 minutes from freezer to plate. Added to a robust stew or soup, tomato sauce can soothe the harshest vagaries of life. I always keep a supply on hand in the freezer. It's a good idea to place portions of the sauce – based on ½ cup (125 ml) per serving – into zip-lock bags for freezing.*

Miso-Garlic Broth and Gravy

Makes 5 cups (1.25 L)

1 Tb	vegetable oil	15 mL
1 cup	onions, diced	250 mL
2 Tb	garlic, minced	30 mL
2 Tb	ginger, minced	30 mL
¼ cup	miso	50 mL
4 cups	vegetable stock (p 7/8) or water	1 L
2 Tb	sweet soy sauce (p 18)	30 mL

1 In a saucepan, heat oil. Add onions, garlic and ginger. Sauté over medium-high heat for 3 to 4 minutes, or until onions start to brown. Add miso and stir well until a smooth paste is formed. Add stock and sweet soy sauce and bring the mixture to a boil. Reduce the heat and simmer uncovered for 10 minutes.

2 Pour the broth into a clean pot and place on a wire rack. Cool to room temperature, then refrigerate overnight. Will keep refrigerated for 2 to 3 days and frozen for 1 month.

MISO-GARLIC GRAVY

In a saucepan over medium heat, bring 2 cups (500 mL) of miso-garlic broth to a boil. In a cup, mix together 2 Tb (30 mL) of cornstarch and an equal amount of water. Add the cornstarch mixture to the broth, stirring until the broth thickens. Serve the gravy at once over steamed rice or vegetables.

Miso *is both a nutritious and flavourful addition to your diet. With a little thickening, the broth makes a general-purpose sauce similar to gravy and enlivens many starch and grain dishes. To dress up the broth or gravy, add roasted garlic cloves or sautéed mushrooms.*

Roasted Garlic Confit

Makes 2 cups (500 mL) oil and garlic
Oven at 350°F (180°C)

1 cup	vegetable oil	250 mL
1 cup	whole garlic cloves, peeled (about 4 whole heads)	250 mL

1 In an ovenproof skillet or small sauce-pan, heat oil. Cook the garlic cloves over medium-high heat until they start to bub-ble. Place in the oven and roast for 10 to 15 minutes, or until the garlic cloves are golden brown and slightly puffed.

2 Remove from the oven and cool to room temperature. Transfer to a covered storage container and refrigerate. Use either whole garlic cloves or the infused oil to add rich flavour to any dish. Will keep refrigerated for 1 or 2 days. (WARNING: Storing garlic cloves in oil presents a potential health risk. Botulism spores are often present in the mixture, and the lack of oxygen in the oil-covered cloves makes an ideal environment for the development of botulism. For this reason, the garlic confit *must* be used within 1 or 2 days.)

The slow poaching of garlic in oil makes two handy and tasty products. The garlic cloves are soft, nutty and richly flavoured. The oil is infused with a mellow garlic flavour that is perfect for use in salad dressings, as well as for cooking, for marinating vegetables or for drizzling over mashed potatoes.

Homemade Curry Paste

Makes about 1 cup (250 mL)

2 Tb	vegetable oil	30 mL
1 Tb	ginger, minced	15 mL
1 Tb	garlic, minced	15 mL
1	onion, diced	1
1 tsp	ground cloves	5 mL
1 tsp	cayenne	5 mL
1 tsp	ground nutmeg	5 mL
1 Tb	ground coriander	15 mL
	Salt and pepper to taste	
2 Tb	ground turmeric	30 mL
	Additional vegetable oil	

1 In a nonstick skillet, heat oil. Add ginger and garlic. Sauté over medium-high heat for about 1 minute, until fragrant. Add onion, ground cloves, cayenne, ground nutmeg, ground coriander, salt, pepper and turmeric. (NOTE: if your food processor has a plastic bowl, add the turmeric *after* processing the curry and transferring it to a glass storage container, or else the turmeric will dye the plastic yellow.) Mix well and sauté for 3 to 4 minutes, or until onion is soft and the spices are highly aromatic.

2 Transfer the mixture to a food processor or blender. Purée until a smooth paste is formed, adding additional vegetable oil if necessary. Transfer to a covered glass jar, let cool and refrigerate. Will keep refrigerated for 1 month.

The flavours of curry are greatly enhanced when freshly roasted spices are used, as the heat of pan-roasting activates their aromatic oils. Indian restaurants often make a fresh curry mix each day to ensure optimum flavour in their cooking. The curry powder is best when used within 1 month. Curry paste has a much longer shelf life, as the oil is infused with the fresh spice flavour.

Homemade Curry Powder

Makes about 1 cup (250 mL)

1 tsp	whole cloves	5 mL
2 Tb	whole coriander seeds	30 mL
2 Tb	whole cumin seeds	30 mL
2 Tb	whole mustard seeds	30 mL
1 tsp	black peppercorns	5 mL
1 tsp	cayenne	5 mL
1 tsp	ground nutmeg	5 mL
2 Tb	ground turmeric	30 mL
2 Tb	powdered ginger	30 mL
2 Tb	garlic powder	30 mL
2 Tb	onion powder	30 mL

1 In a dry skillet, combine cloves, coriander seeds, cumin seeds, mustard seeds and peppercorns. Heat until the spices are aromatic, about 1 minute.

2 Transfer the mixture to a spice grinder (or use a mortar and pestle) and grind to a fine powder. Add the remaining ingredients and pulse to mix. Transfer to a covered glass jar. Will keep for 1 month.

Ginger-Citrus Syrup

Makes 2 cups (500 L)

1 cup	sugar (or honey)	250 mL
1 cup	water	250 mL
½ cup	ginger, sliced	125 mL
Juice and zest of 1 lemon		
Juice and zest of 1 grapefruit		
1 Tb	cornstarch	15 mL
(dissolved in equal amount of water)		

1 In a small saucepan, combine sugar, water, ginger, and juice and zest of lemon and grapefruit. Bring to a boil, then reduce the heat and simmer uncovered for 15 minutes. Remove any scum that floats to the surface. Add cornstarch mixture and stir for about 1 minute, or until syrup thickens.

2 Remove from the heat and cool to room temperature. Transfer to a covered glass jar and refrigerate. Will keep refrigerated for up to 2 months. (NOTE: This mixture does not freeze well.)

Ginger and lemon are a tasty combination, and this syrup is a welcome addition to salad dressings, sauces or a cup of tea. A teaspoonful (5 ml) of the mixture dissolved in a cup (250 ml) of hot water is reported to lessen the symptoms of chest colds and boost the body's immune system.

Bottled Sauces, Oils and Vinegars

Bottled sauces and condiments are a great convenience in our modern lives. They are available from countries all over the world and will add an authentic taste to any dish you make. Look for sauces that are free of (or low in) monosodium glutamate (MSG) and salt. Many bottled sauces are a healthy and handy way to infuse your cooking with different flavours.

Soy Sauces and Miso

Soy sauces have been produced from soybeans for thousands of years. The finer varieties are aged like fine wine in cedar and oak barrels. Chinese in origin, soy sauce has spread to many Pacific Rim countries and is fully integrated into their cuisines.

Light Soy Sauce

The least aged and lightest tasting of the soy sauces, this one is excellent for salad dressings and as a table condiment for rice. Low-sodium varieties are available. The finest quality light soy sauce generally comes from Japan and has a winelike aroma and slightly yeasty flavour.

Tamari Sauce

Tamari is a light soy sauce, developed in Japan, that is often made without the addition of wheat (check the label for details). This makes it suitable for use by people with allergies to wheat and gluten. Sometimes barley or rice is used in the preparation to add flavour and body to the sauce.

Dark Soy Sauce

Dark and full-bodied, this sauce packs a high salt content and has a deep rich flavour. It is mainly used for braising and flavouring sauces and dips, and imparts a deep mahogany colour to vegetables.

Soy Paste

A fairly recent addition to the market, soy paste is richly flavoured and thickened with the addition of starch. It can be added directly to vegetables and is also tasty on stir-fried noodles.

Mushroom Soy Sauce

This is dark soy sauce enhanced with the addition of shiitake or straw mushrooms. The rich flavour complements mushroom dishes. A thickened version of the sauce is sometimes labelled Vegetarian Oyster Sauce.

Sweet Soy Sauce

This soy sauce, sweetened with cane sugar, is sold in many Asian markets, sometimes under the name Kecap Manis (Indonesian soy sauce). It is used for cooking and is also excellent drizzled directly over rice, noodles, mushrooms or steamed vegetables. If you cannot find it, here is a recipe for a fair substitute that you can make at home:

HOMEMADE SWEET SOY SAUCE

1 cup	dark soy sauce	250 mL
2 Tb	brown sugar	30 mL
1 Tb	dark molasses	15 mL

1 Place dark soy sauce, brown sugar and molasses in a small container that has a lid. Stir well to dissolve the sugar.

2 Cover and store in the refrigerator. Will keep refrigerated for 1 month.

Miso

Miso is a Japanese product that is fermented soybean paste, often with the addition of rice, brown rice or barley. Miso is aged in cedar barrels to various degrees of flavour, colour and saltiness. The older it is, the darker the colour, the stronger the flavour and the higher the salt content. Light (or white) miso is fruity and yeasty, with a slightly sweet flavour. Yellow or light brown miso is a little stronger and saltier, and adds a deeper dimension of flavour to a dish. Red or dark brown miso is the most aged and pungent. Use aged miso in smaller quantities to compensate for the higher salt level and stronger flavour.

Cooking Sauces and Condiments

In the past few years, there has been an explosion in the number and type of sauces – many of them hot sauces – available from around the world. Thousands of manufacturers offer products in many different styles. These are some of my favourites.

Black Bean Sauce

This Chinese aromatic paste is a pungent and salty mixture of fermented black soybeans, sometimes with garlic and ginger. It is a tasty addition to stir-fries and makes an excellent addition to sauces for broccoli, cauliflower, cabbage and many Asian vegetables.

Char Sui Sauce

Char sui is a sugar-based sauce infused with spices. The bottle is often labelled Chinese Barbecue Sauce. Satay sauce is related but is made with the addition of curry spices, chilis and lots of oil. Char sui sauce makes an intriguing addition to sauces and stir-fries.

Chili Sauce

The hottest sauces are made from serrano, Thai bird's-eye or habanero chilies. Chili sauce is available combined with a number of other ingredients, such as garlic, ginger or onions. Another variation is sweet chili sauce, made by adding sugar syrup, and it is excellent on pan-fried tofu slices.

Chili-Bean Paste

Several types of chili paste are available with the added pungency of fermented beans. The bean paste used is made either from yellow fermented soybeans or fermented black beans. The combination of fermented bean paste and intense chili oil can be extremely hot.

Chili Vinegar

Many vinegar-based chili sauces are available from Thailand, Vietnam and Indonesia. The traditional Tabasco sauce is an example of puréed chili-vinegar sauce. Look for the type of pepper on the label: jalapeño (moderate) and serrano (hot) will be kinder than the explosive habanero (very hot).

Curry

Curry is a mixture of spices made in countless variations. Of the commonly available varieties, Madras curry is suited for the widest array of dishes. Bottled curry pastes last quite a long time and are a convenient way to give dishes an instant burst of flavour. Dry curry powders tend to lose many of their aromatic components over time. The best curries are made by pan-roasting whole spices and grinding them just before use.

Hoisin Sauce

This thick, rich sauce is often made from puréed yam, spices and soy sauce. It can be added to salad dressings and can also be used to flavour mustard or mayonnaise used in sandwiches and wraps.

Mustard

Many types of mustard are available. Everyday yellow mustard is mild and tangy, and blends well with soy and hoisin sauces. Dijon mustard has a vinegary bite and can be quite hot. Grainy mustard has the extra zip of whole mustard seeds. All mustards make good additions to salad dressings and are sublime with potatoes.

Plum Sauce

Plum sauce is a sweet and sour combination of plums, vinegar, ginger and chilies. It is fine on its own as a dipping sauce or as an addition to dressings and sauces. The flavour can be enlivened by a squeeze of fresh lemon or lime juice.

Wasabi

Wasabi is a Japanese condiment that is hot and pungent, similar to horseradish or mustard. True wasabi is produced from a rare root found in alpine lakes in Japan. Most commercial wasabi is powdered horseradish with green food colouring. Mix the wasabi powder with a little water to form a thick paste (be careful not to breathe in the powder or get it near your eyes). Wasabi is also available premixed into a paste in handy tubes. To make a tasty dipping sauce for sushi, each person should add a pea-sized lump of wasabi paste to 2 tablespoons (30 mL) of light or Japanese soy sauce and stir to mix well.

Oils

Oil plays a key role in the cooking process by helping salt, seasonings and herbs to cling to vegetables and allowing flavours to penetrate evenly. Oil is composed of fat in the form of saturated, monounsaturated and polyunsaturated fats. Each of us deals with and metabolizes calories and cholesterol (a basic building block of cell structure) at different rates. Saturated fats are the ones to avoid; they occur mainly in animal fats and some vegetable products like coconut oil. Cholesterol is found in all dairy products, but rarely in plants (coconut and avocado contain a form of cholesterol).

All-Purpose Vegetable Oils

The all-round choice for cooking oil is probably canola, which is high in polyunsaturated fats and low in cholesterol. It also has one of the highest burning points and is well suited to all types of cooking. Since it is fairly neutral in taste, canola is a good oil for salad dressings and other preparations that require a clear, light oil. Canola was one of the first crops to be manipulated through genetic engineering; if this idea bothers you, seek out organically grown canola oil or purchase a brand that is labelled as being made from genetically unaltered plants. Other good vegetable oils for all-round use are sunflower, corn and safflower.

Olive Oil

The virtues of olive oil have been praised for centuries. The Mediterranean diet, based on lashings of olive oil and wine, has been acclaimed as a healthy way to live. Olive oil is monounsaturated and is sold in many grades and prices.

Light olive oil is the least expensive and is suitable for all-round cooking. Pomace oil is slightly higher in quality, costs a bit more and contains a higher percentage of organic matter (making it unsuitable for high-temperature applications). It is a full-bodied addition to salad dressings and is good for use in a quick sauté.

Extra-virgin is the best commonly available olive oil. Cold-pressed olive oil is the finest and most expensive grade of extra-virgin. The best ones are from Italy and California, and are often designated with the name of the olive grove, much like expensive wines. Extra-virgin olive oil contains a high amount of organic matter and has a fairly low burning point, so should not be used for high-heat cooking. Its delicate flavour is best enjoyed drizzled over salads and breads.

Sesame Oil

Made from toasted sesame seeds, this oil adds a wonderful nutty flavour to foods. The oil has a very low burning point, so it is used for flavouring, not cooking. The best quality sesame oils are from Japan. Avoid those that are dark in colour and murky.

Vinegars

Vinegar was originally made from wine that had gone sour. Today, specialty vinegars are made from apple cider, white wine, red wine, sherry or rice wine – or flavoured with herbs or fruits. I use organic apple cider vinegar for many salad dressings (cider vinegar is a well-known aid to digestion).

All-Purpose White Vinegar

Plain white vinegar works well for cooking and dressings. It's also handy as a kitchen cleaner. After washing my cutting boards, I splash them with vinegar to destroy surface bacteria and eliminate odours.

Balsamic Vinegar

Balsamic vinegar is a gastronomic delight. It is made from the reduced juice of Trebbiano grapes and aged in a succession of wooden barrels for many years (up to a hundred). A key process is the addition of older batches of vinegar to younger ones, to produce a smooth rich blend. The oldest balsamic vinegars may be drunk like fine liqueurs and are labelled Aceto Balsamico Tradizionale. Most commercially available versions are blends of bulk vinegar mixed with varying degrees of true balsamic vinegar. The cheaper ones may also be doctored with caramel colouring, but they still have a pleasant flavour. As a treat, spend at least ten dollars on a small bottle and splash a little of it over fresh strawberries – pure magic!

Rice Vinegar

Rice vinegar is a low-acid vinegar that is used in many Asian-flavoured dishes. It is generally clear, light flavoured and aromatic.

HERBS FOR FLAVOURING

Fresh herbs play an essential role in fine cooking, particularly in vegetarian cuisine. Herbs have been gathered for both culinary and medicinal use since the dawn of civilization. Many common herbs such as parsley, mint, sage, oregano, thyme and rosemary are native to southern Europe (mainly the Mediterranean region) and have been exported and cultivated around the world. Basil is believed to be native to India, where it is an important plant in the Hindu religion (often referred to as holy basil). Herbs contain many volatile aromatic components, but these oils and flavours are altered when the plant is dried. Dried herbs are usually a pale shadow of the fresh ones and generally add a tannic and oxidized flavour. Marjoram, thyme, sage and rosemary are among the few herbs that produce a reasonable dried product.

Basil *(Ocimum basilicum)*

Basil escaped its roots in India and travelled to all points on the globe. Italian, Thai and Vietnamese cooks have embraced basil as their own, using it in dressings, soups, curries and tomato sauces. The pungent and volatile flavours do not dry well. There are dozens of varieties of basil – globe, bush, mint, chocolate and lemon basil are all worth cultivating for the subtle differences in flavour.

Chives *(Allium schoenoprasum)*

A welcome herald of spring, chive stems and flowers provide a tasty, elegant garnish for many dishes. The stems can also be used to tie together bundles of vegetables (like asparagus) for steaming or blanching.

Cilantro *(Coriandrum sativum)*

Known by many names including Chinese parsley and leaf coriander, cilantro is a pungently flavoured herb that is best used in moderation. Add it at the end of cooking to obtain the full fragrance. The seeds of the plant are also used in cooking and are commonly called coriander seeds.

Garlic *(Allium sativum)*

Evidence from as far back as 2000 B.C. records the cultivation of garlic in ancient Egypt and Mesopotamia. Garlic is used in stir-fries, sauces, soups, dressings and stocks. Scientific studies have identified an active component, allins, that may protect against cancer and cardiovascular disease. The consumption of raw garlic may lower blood cholesterol levels and reduce blood clotting. Garlic is a proven mild antiseptic and is believed to contribute to the overall well-being of our immune systems.

Ginger (*Zingiber officinale*)

Native to southwest Asia, ginger was an important food and medicine for the ancient Greeks and Romans. Ginger is used as a flavouring, an aromatic and as an important source of minerals and vitamins. Research has indicated that ginger has important antibacterial and antioxidant properties. A syrup made from ginger is widely used as a mild antifungal and antibacterial tonic. It also helps clean the blood of impurities and saturated fats, and may play an important role in nutrient absorption and general digestion.

Mint (*Mentha sp.*)

There are reputed to be hundreds of varieties of mint available; the best known are peppermint, spearmint and applemint. It is an aid to digestion and widely utilized as a refreshing tea, as well as to flavour medicines and desserts.

Oregano or Wild Marjoram (*Origanum vulgare*)

Another herb used by the ancient Greeks and Romans, oregano grows wild in many parts of the world. It has a special affinity for tomatoes and is the main herb in many tomato sauces. The dried version lacks many of the volatile components that give the fresh herb its fragrance and flavour.

Parsley (*Petroselinum crispum*)

One of the most widely used herbs in the world, parsley was scattered around Europe by the Romans. The curly leaf variety is the most common, but other varieties include the flat leaf, which imparts a slight celery flavour to dishes. Parsley is an excellent source of vitamin C and is said to cleanse the palate and aid in digestion.

Rosemary (*Rosmarinus officinalis*)

A personal favourite, rosemary is an aromatic herb that has many applications in cooking, aromatherapy and medicine. A stem of rosemary can be used whole to baste vegetables on the grill. The woody stems may be stripped of leaves and used as flavourful skewers to grill vegetables and mushrooms. Rosemary has a special affinity for potatoes and is also excellent in cheese dishes. Rosemary can be used fresh or dried.

Sage (*Salvia officinalis*)

Native to the Mediterranean, sage is best known for its use in stuffing, but it is used commercially to flavour sausages, cheeses and beverages. In the spring, the plant produces beautiful flowers that are delicious in a mixed green salad. A number of strongly scented varieties are available, including the fragrant pineapple sage. Try adding sage to iced tea.

Thyme (*Thymus vulgaris*)

Thyme is renowned for its medicinal qualities as well as its culinary uses. The essential oil of the plant contains a mild antiseptic, used in many preparations. The hardy herb has many fragrant varieties, including the wonderful lemon thyme. Thyme is a good choice for dishes that contain onions, and it is used in many soups, dressings, sauces and stews.

Unusual Herbs

Relatively few herbs are commercially available – there are dozens more for the adventurous to try. The best way to take advantage of the many varieties is to grow them yourself. Whether you have a garden plot, a window planter or containers on your patio, fresh herbs will add joy and flavour to your life. Many herbs can be added to salads or steeped in boiling water to make a delicious tea. Here are some herbs to seek out in the seed and bedding plant sections of your local nursery:

Anise Hyssop (*Agastache foeniculum*)
Bergamot (*Monarda didyma*)
Chervil (*Anthriscus cerefolium*)
English Lavender (*Lavandula augustifolia*)
Lemon Balm (*Melissa officinalis*)
Lemon Verbena (*Aloysia triphylla*)
Lovage (*Levisticum officinale*)
Nasturtium (*Tropaeolum majus*)
Salad Burnet (*Poterium sanguisorba*)
Scented Geranium (*Pelargonium spp.*)
Shiso (*Perilla frutescens*)
Sweet Cicely (*Crithmum maritimum*)

WINE AND VEGETARIAN CUISINE

Matching wines with vegetarian dishes is easier than you might think. Many of the same rules apply as for matching meats, poultry and seafood. In general, the seasoning, sauces and cooking methods have a bearing on the types of wine that will taste good with a dish. When wine truly compliments food, it usually results from a balance of flavour and acidity. Creamy foods like goat's cheese or flavourful roasted vegetables pair well with a full-bodied wine like a Cabernet Sauvignon. Foods with a higher fat content like butter and cream are complemented by a rich, complex wine like an oak-matured Chardonnay. Ice wines are perfect when balanced by a sharp, citrus-based dessert.

The flavours of wines are mainly defined by the grape type. The winemaker's skill, contribution of the vineyard soil and climate are the other modifying factors. When you drink a wine, certain aromatic characteristics come forward on the nose (scent) and taste of the wine. Some are herbal (thyme, mint, eucalyptus), others are fruit (citrus, berries, apples, pears), or vegetable (pepper, asparagus, melon) and even mineral (metallic, steel, flint). Wines with such characteristics will match food that shares some of the same qualities.

Contrast is another key concept to choosing wines. Instead of matching flavours, sometimes opposite flavours and qualities combine to form a harmonious balance. Dishes flavoured with complex Indian spices (like curry) are good paired with a simple, floral wine like a Riesling or Pinot Gris. Asian foods, especially Chinese and Japanese dishes (based on soy, garlic and ginger), are best with a Chenin Blanc or Gewürztraminer. Thousands of wines are available for your drinking and dining pleasure – so relax, experiment and enjoy the journey.

White Wines

Chardonnay

Medium to full bodied, aged in oak or stainless steel. An aroma of apples, citrus, butterscotch, vanilla and tropical fruit. Good with pasta, potato or mushroom dishes that feature cream or cheese. Also good with dishes that include aromatic and slightly licorice-flavoured herbs like tarragon, fennel, chervil and sweet cicely. An excellent all-round choice.

Chenin Blanc

Light to medium bodied, available from off-dry to semisweet. The aroma of flowers, apples, melons, ripe pears and peaches is balanced by a fresh smooth taste. Perfect for vegetarian sushi and sauces with a ginger, garlic or soy base. A pleasant foil to spicy Thai and Indonesian dishes. Great as an appetizer.

Gewürztraminer

Light to medium bodied, available from bone-dry to dessert styles. A spicy aroma of tropical fruit, citrus, rose and minerals. The rich, complex flavour complements powerfully seasoned and spiced dishes like curries and Thai stir-fries. The dessert variety is delicious with caramelized tropical fruits like lychee and mango.

Pinot Blanc

Light to medium bodied, generally very dry. The steely aroma of green apples and pears is balanced by a gently herbal and floral nose and fresh flavour. A good match with roasted or caramelized onions and garlic. Drink with dishes containing nuts, mild cheeses, yogurt or sour cream. A good food wine that cleanses the palate.

Riesling

Light to medium bodied, available as semi-sweet, dry, late harvest and dessert (ice) wine. A delicate and aromatic blend of flowers, citrus, melon, herbs and minerals. This versatile wine works well with appetizers, fried foods, pasta, stir-fries and salads, particularly dishes with citrus-based dressings and sauces.

Sauvignon Blanc

Light to medium bodied, generally bone dry. An aroma of herbs, dried hay, green pepper, asparagus, gooseberry and green apple. A perfect wine for appetizers, salads, pastas, noodles and a wide array of light vegetable dishes. Goes very well with tomato-based dishes and is a classic match with goat's cheese and fresh herbs.

Red Wines

Cabernet Franc

Medium to full bodied, mild tannin and an aroma of cherry, cedar, dried herbs and blackberry. A good food wine that pairs well with mushrooms, cheese and grilled or cream-based dishes. An excellent all-round wine.

Cabernet Sauvignon

Medium to full bodied, tannic and dry. The aroma contains elements of blackcurrant (cassis), pepper, herbs, tobacco, cedar and mint. Demands strong flavours to stand up to it: tomato-based dishes, goat's cheese, aged cheeses (such as Parmesan), blue cheese and grilled or roasted vegetables.

Merlot

Medium to full bodied, dry with soft tannins. An aroma of ripe black cherries, raspberries, citrus and gentle floral. Similar to Cabernet Sauvignon but softer and gentler. The best wine for braised dishes, all types of cheeses, rustic pasta and roasted vegetables.

Pinot Noir

Light to medium bodied, low tannin and smooth textured. An aroma of cherries, violet, earth (barnyard), smoke and wildflowers. Goes well with barbecued foods, wild mushrooms, cream, soft cheeses (such as Camembert or brie), lightly spiced curries and Middle Eastern flavours. An all-round red wine for sipping and dining.

Shiraz (Syrah)

Medium to full bodied, with firm tannins and a spicy nose. An aroma of ripe berry fruit, black pepper, spice, mint and tobacco. Drink with caramelized onions or slightly charred, grilled, sautéed or roasted vegetables.

Zinfandel

Medium to full bodied, ranges from spicy and pungent to light and floral. An aroma of ripe berry fruit (blackberry, raspberry), black pepper, spicy, leather and licorice. Perfect for a summer barbecue, spicy tomato-based dishes, hearty stews, pizza and anything with roasted red peppers.

Appetizers

Caramelized Onion and Garlic Hummus with Pan-fried Pita

Serves 4
Oven at 200°F (100°C)

Onion and Garlic Hummus

1 Tb	olive oil	15 mL
2	onions, thinly sliced	2
1 Tb	garlic, minced	15 mL
1 Tb	honey	15 mL
	Salt and pepper to taste	
¼ cup	dry white wine (or apple juice)	50 mL
2 cups	canned chickpeas, drained, reserve liquid	500 mL
(or dried chickpeas, simmered 2 hours in water)		
½ cup	cooking liquid from chickpeas	125 mL
	Juice of 1 lemon	
2 Tb	garlic, minced	30 mL
1 tsp	hot sauce (or to taste)	5 mL
2 Tb	chives (or parsley or cilantro), minced	30 mL
	Salt and pepper to taste	

Pan-fried Pita

1 Tb	olive oil	15 mL
4	large pita breads	4
	Chopped chives (or parsley) for garnish	

1   In a nonstick skillet, heat olive oil. Over medium-high heat, sauté onions and garlic for about 5 minutes, or until onions begin to brown, then add honey. Season with salt and pepper. Stir well and cook for 5 to 7 minutes, or until the onions start to caramelize. Add the white wine and cook over high heat for 5 minutes, or until the moisture has evaporated and the onions are golden brown.

2   In a blender or food processor, combine caramelized onions, cooked chickpeas, cooking liquid, lemon juice and garlic. Purée, stopping as needed to clean the sides of the bowl with a spatula. If necessary, thin with more cooking liquid to make a smooth soft paste. Season with hot sauce, herbs, salt and pepper, stirring well.

3   Place another nonstick skillet over medium heat for 1 minute. Brush or drizzle a little of the olive oil on a pita bread and pan-fry in the skillet for 3 to 4 minutes per side, or until golden brown, then keep warm in the oven. Repeat with remaining pita breads.

4   To serve, transfer pita breads to a cutting board and cut into wedges. Place the hummus in a small serving bowl, set it in the middle of a large platter, and surround it with the warm pita wedges. Garnish with chopped chives.

Try some other flavour variations: for the onions, substitute avocado or puréed leftover cold vegetables (broccoli, spinach, roasted red pepper or yam are particularly good). For the pita, substitute any thin round flatbread such as focaccia or naan.

Tortilla Wrap Stuffed with Goat's Cheese, Tomato, Arugula and Sunflower Seeds

Serves 4

4	large tortillas (white, whole wheat or flavoured)	4
1 cup	arugula, shredded	250 mL
1 cup	lettuce, shredded	250 mL
1	tomato, diced	1
1 Tb	extra-virgin olive oil	15 mL
	Salt and pepper to taste	
½ cup	soft goat's cheese	125 mL
¼ cup	toasted sunflower seeds (shelled)	50 mL

1 Place a dry nonstick skillet over medium-high heat for 1 minute. Dry-cook tortillas one at a time for 1 or 2 minutes per side, or until lightly browned. Set aside on a platter and keep warm.

2 In a bowl, combine arugula, lettuce and tomato. Drizzle with extra-virgin olive oil and season with salt and pepper. Toss to mix well.

3 Lay one tortilla on a work surface. Spread ¼ of the cheese on one half of the tortilla. Sprinkle ¼ of the sunflower seeds over the cheese. Heap ¼ of the salad mix in a line across the cheese, near the middle of the tortilla. Fold the empty half of the tortilla over the filling and gently squeeze into a tight log. Roll the wrap into a tight cylinder. (The tortillas can be stuffed 1 to 2 hours in advance, individually wrapped in plastic cling wrap and refrigerated.)

4 To serve, remove the cling wrap and cut into slices 1 inch (2.5 cm) thick. Arrange on a platter.

You can *use many substitutions for the filling ingredients, but you will need a soft mild cheese to act as a binder for the filling. For a more substantial snack, add more lettuce and arugula, loosely roll up the wraps and serve whole.*

Pan-fried Dumplings Stuffed with Sui Choy and Mushrooms

Serves 4 to 8
Oven at 200°F (100°C)

1 oz	bean thread noodles	30 g
1	small wood ear fungus	1
4	dried shiitake mushrooms	4
2 slices	ginger	2 slices
1 Tb	vegetable oil	15 mL
2 Tb	ginger, minced	30 mL
1 cup	sui choy (Chinese cabbage), shredded	250 mL
1 Tb	sweet soy sauce (p 18)	15 mL
1 tsp	hot sauce (or to taste)	5 mL
1 tsp	sesame oil	5 mL
24	store-bought round won ton wrappers	24
1	egg, beaten with 1 tsp/5 mL water	1
1 Tb	vegetable oil (second amount)	15 mL

SOY-VINEGAR DIPPING SAUCE

2 Tb	sweet soy sauce (p 18)	30 mL
1 Tb	lemon juice	15 mL
1 Tb	hot sauce (or to taste)	15 mL
½ cup	white wine (or rice) vinegar	125 mL

The *moist filling requires that the dumplings be made just before cooking. You can prepare the filling in advance and involve family and friends in the dumpling production line.*

1 In a heatproof bowl, combine bean thread noodles, wood ear fungus, shiitake mushrooms and ginger slices. Cover with boiling water and soak for 10 minutes. Remove the mushrooms from the broth, cut off and discard the stems, and dice the caps. Place in a bowl and set aside. Strain the noodles (reserving ½ cup/125 mL of the broth) and place in a separate bowl. Use scissors to cut the noodles into small pieces.

2 In a nonstick skillet, heat vegetable oil. Sauté minced ginger over medium-high heat for about 1 minute, or until fragrant. Add sui choy, mushrooms and reserved broth. Season with sweet soy sauce, hot sauce and sesame oil, then bring to a boil. Remove from the heat, mix into the noodles, and allow to cool slightly.

3 Lay out the won ton wrappers on a work surface. With a pastry brush, coat each won ton wrapper with a light covering of beaten egg and water. Place 1 teaspoon (5 mL) of the filling in the centre of each wrapper and fold to form a half moon. Press the edges together and make three small crimps along the edge to really seal the dumplings.

4 In another nonstick skillet, heat vegetable oil (second amount) over medium-high heat for 30 seconds. Pan-fry the won tons, 8 at a time, for 2 to 3 minutes per side, or until golden. Transfer to a paper towel-covered plate (can be kept warm in the oven for up to 30 minutes).

5 In a small serving bowl, mix together sweet soy sauce, lemon juice, hot sauce and white wine vinegar. Let sit for 5 minutes.

6 To serve, arrange the dumplings on a platter, with the soy-vinegar dipping sauce on the side.

Hazelnut Phyllo Bundles Stuffed with Asparagus and Brie

Serves 4 to 8
Oven at 400°F (200°C)

½ lb	asparagus, trimmed	250 g
1 Tb	garlic, minced	15 mL
	Juice and zest of 1 lemon	
	Salt and pepper to taste	
4 sheets	store-bought phyllo pastry	4 sheets
¼ cup	hazelnuts, toasted and crushed	50 mL
	Baking spray (or melted butter)	
4 oz	brie, thinly sliced	125 g
	Whole lettuce leaves for wrapping	

Frozen phyllo pastry is sold in most supermarkets. The trick to using phyllo pastry is to keep it moist by covering with a damp, clean kitchen towel, until you need it. Try to fold any cracked areas of the phyllo into the bundle, leaving a clean unbroken surface for your final fold. Once the bundles are made, brush well with butter or oil to keep them from drying out and cracking; they will keep for 2 to 3 hours in the refrigerator before being baked.

1   Bring a stockpot filled with salted water to a boil. Add asparagus and cook for 2 to 3 minutes, or until bright green and tender. Remove asparagus from water and plunge into a bowl of ice and cold water. When cool, drain asparagus and place on a paper towel-lined plate. Cut into sections 2 inches (5 cm) long and place in a small bowl, then add garlic, lemon juice and zest. Season with salt and pepper, then mix well. Set aside.

2   Lay two sheets of phyllo pastry on a work surface. Place the remaining sheets under a damp kitchen towel. Oil the surface of one phyllo sheet with baking spray and sprinkle evenly with ½ of the crushed hazelnuts. Top with the second phyllo sheet and oil with baking spray. Use a sharp knife to cut the layered phyllo into squares 4 × 4 inches (10 × 10 cm). Repeat with the remaining phyllo sheets, oil and hazelnuts.

3   Place 2 or 3 spears of asparagus near the bottom edge of a phyllo square. Place thin slices of brie on the asparagus. Fold the bottom edge of the phyllo over the filling, mould into a tight log, then roll up into a tight cylinder. Moisten the top edge of the phyllo with baking spray and press lightly to seal. Repeat with the remaining phyllo squares and filling. (Can be prepared ahead and refrigerated for 2 to 3 hours. Coat lightly with baking spray to prevent drying.)

4   Place the rolls seam-side down on a baking sheet and oil with baking spray. Bake in the oven for 15 minutes, or until golden brown and crispy.

5   To serve, place whole lettuce leaves on a platter. Cut the phyllo bundles in half and arrange them beside the lettuce. To eat, take a lettuce leaf and wrap it around half of a phyllo bundle, then eat it out of the hand.

Vietnamese-style Salad Rolls with Cilantro–Pumpkin Seed Pesto

Serves 4

CILANTRO–PUMPKIN SEED PESTO

½ cup	toasted pumpkin seeds (shelled)	125 mL
¼ cup	cilantro, chopped	50 mL
½ cup	spinach leaves	125 mL
1 tsp	honey	5 mL
1 Tb	ginger, minced	15 mL
2 Tb	vegetable oil	30 mL
2 Tb	apple juice (or water)	30 mL
	Salt and pepper to taste	

SALAD ROLLS

2 oz	rice noodles	60 g
1	carrot, julienned	1
½	cucumber, seeded and julienned	½
1	zucchini, seeded and julienned	1
1 cup	bean sprouts	250 mL
8	small disks of rice paper	8

Rice paper disks are very fragile when dry, but they become pliable when soaked in hot water. The hotter the water, the more quickly the rice paper will soften. If left to soak for too long, the sheets become too soft. For best results, soak and use one sheet at a time, working quickly.

1   In a blender or food processor, combine pumpkin seeds, cilantro, spinach, honey, ginger and vegetable oil. Purée to a slightly coarse mixture and thin with apple juice to make a fairly smooth paste. Season with salt and pepper. Set aside.

2   Place rice noodles in a heatproof bowl and cover with boiling water. Let sit for 5 minutes, or until the noodles become soft and pliable. Drain the noodles and use scissors to cut into bite-size chunks. Set aside.

3   In a bowl, combine carrot, cucumber, zucchini and bean sprouts. Add half of the pesto mixture and toss to coat well.

4   Fill a shallow heatproof pan with 1 inch (2.5 cm) of boiling water. Place one disk of rice paper in the hot water and allow to soften for 30 seconds (slightly longer as the water cools). Gently remove the rice paper, drain and place on a flat work surface.

5   Place a heaping row of rice noodles down the centre of the rice paper. Top with a little of the pesto and sprinkle with 1/8 of the marinated vegetables. Fold one side of the rice paper over the filling and squeeze into a tight log. Fold the top and bottom of the rice paper over each end of the log, then roll into a tight cylinder. Repeat with the remaining rice paper and filling. (Can be prepared ahead and refrigerated for 2 to 3 hours.)

6   To serve, cut each roll in half on an angle and arrange on a platter.

Lettuce Wraps
Stuffed with Roasted Yam and Tofu

Serves 4
Oven at 350°F (180°C)

2 cups	small yams, peeled and diced	500 mL
1 cup	firm tofu, finely diced	250 mL
2 Tb	olive oil	30 mL
1 Tb	garlic, minced	15 mL
1 Tb	ginger, minced	15 mL
1 tsp	hot sauce (or to taste)	5 mL
	Salt and pepper to taste	
1 head	iceberg lettuce	1 head
¼ cup	hoisin sauce	50 mL
¼ cup	basil (or cilantro)	50 mL

1 In a bowl, combine yams and tofu. Add olive oil, garlic, ginger and hot sauce. Season well with salt and pepper. Toss to coat and transfer to a roasting pan. Roast in the oven for 20 to 30 minutes, or until yams are tender and beginning to brown. Remove from the oven and set aside to cool slightly.

2 Prepare lettuce by removing the hard core of the head and separating the large leaves.

3 To serve, place hoisin sauce in a small serving bowl and set on a large platter. Stack the lettuce leaves on one side of the platter and mound the filling on the other side. Stack basil leaves next to the lettuce.

4 To eat, take a lettuce leaf and spread a little hoisin sauce on it. Add a spoonful of the filling and a leaf or two of basil. Roll up the lettuce leaf into a cylinder and eat it out of the hand.

This is a variation on a classic Chinese dish that usually calls for minced chicken or pork, here replaced with yam and tofu. Yams have a lot of natural sugar; they tend to caramelize (and burn) quickly, so keep an eye on them.

Potato Canapés with Cambozola Cheese and Roasted Garlic Cloves

Serves 6 to 8

1 lb	small nugget potatoes	500 g
4 oz	Cambozola cheese	125 g
4 oz	cream cheese	125 g
2 Tb	chives, chopped	30 mL
	Salt and pepper to taste	
½ cup	garlic cloves	125 mL
	from roasted garlic confit (p 13)	
	Minced chives for garnish	

1 Bring a stockpot filled with salted water to a boil. Add potatoes and cook for 4 to 5 minutes, or until just tender. Remove from the water and plunge into a bowl of cold water and ice. When cool, remove from the water and drain on paper towels.

2 Cut each potato in half. Using a melon baller or small spoon, scoop out some flesh from the centre of each half. Cut a thin slice off the bottom of each potato half to allow it to sit flat. Reserve the potato trimmings.

3 In a blender or food processor, combine the potato trimmings, Cambozola, cream cheese and chives. Purée until a smooth paste is formed. Season with a little salt and a good dose of black pepper.

4 To serve, fill each potato half with the cheese mixture and top with a whole clove of garlic confit. Garnish with a sprinkling of chives.

Spring *and early summer are the prime time for new potatoes. This recipe makes a good party canapé, and pairs well with champagne or a good Chardonnay. For the Cambozola, substitute any blue cheese such as Gorgonzola, Stilton or Roquefort.*

Vegetarian Sushi

Sushi Rice

Makes about 4 cups (1 L)

2 cups	sushi rice	500 mL
3 cups	water	750 mL
1 tsp	sea salt	5 mL
½ cup	rice vinegar	125 mL
⅓ cup	sugar	75 mL
1 tsp	sea salt (second amount)	5 mL

1 Wash rice about 1 hour before you start to cook. Place the rice in a mesh strainer and place that inside a medium bowl. Rinse well with water (rubbing rice gently to release starch) until the rinse water runs clear. Drain rice and let it sit in the strainer for 1 hour.

2 In a heavy saucepan with a lid, combine rice, water and 1 teaspoon (5 mL) sea salt. Let the rice sit for 5 minutes, then turn the heat to high. Bring to a boil, uncovered, then reduce the heat to the lowest setting and cover the pot with a lid. Cook for 20 minutes, or until all the water evaporates. Keep covered (do not peek), remove from the heat and let rest for 20 minutes.

3 In a small bowl, combine rice vinegar, sugar and sea salt (second amount), stirring until dissolved. Transfer the cooked rice to a large shallow pan and spread out evenly. Sprinkle seasoned vinegar over the rice and mix in well. For the next 5 minutes or until cool, stir occasionally to try to separate the rice grains as much as possible and break up any lumps. Cover with a damp, clean kitchen towel. Can be kept at room temperature for 1 to 2 hours before using.

The Japanese secret to perfect rice is to listen to the sound of the rice pot – the rice is done when the sound of steaming stops and a small dry "pop" signals the evaporation of the last bit of water. The real challenge is to not lift up the lid to take a peek while the rice is steaming and resting. The result should be a chewy rice that is soft, plump and sensual.

Japanese Eggplant Sushi

Serves 4 to 6

1 Tb	dark soy sauce	15 mL
1 Tb	honey	15 mL
2 Tb	balsamic vinegar	30 mL
	Salt and pepper	
1	medium Japanese eggplant	1
1 Tb	vegetable oil	15 mL
1 cup	cold water	250 mL
1 tsp	rice vinegar	5 mL
2 cups	cooked sushi rice (p 34)	500 mL
	Wasabi paste	
	Pickled ginger for garnish	
	Soy sauce	

The long, slender Japanese eggplants are seldom bitter like their bigger Mediterranean cousins. A mature eggplant may have bitter components, but these can be removed. First, sprinkle salt over the cut surface of the eggplant, let sit for 5 minutes, then wipe clean with a paper towel. While cooking the eggplant, be careful to keep the temperature moderately hot and to avoid excessive charring.

1 In a bowl, mix together dark soy sauce, honey, balsamic vinegar, salt and pepper. Cut eggplant into slices ½ inch (1 cm) thick. Add eggplant to marinade, tossing well to coat, and let sit for 5 minutes.

2 In a nonstick skillet, heat vegetable oil for 1 minute. Use a slotted spoon to remove the eggplant from the marinade (reserving marinade) and place in the skillet. Cook over medium heat for 5 minutes per side, or until the eggplant is soft and beginning to brown on both sides. Return the eggplant to the marinade and allow to cool to room temperature.

3 In a small bowl, combine water and rice vinegar. With clean hands, dip your fingers into the vinegar water and then scoop up a lump of sushi rice the size of a golf ball. Gently press into a compact ball and place on a platter. Repeat with the remaining rice, while continuing to dip your hands into the vinegar water and wiping them free of rice starch. Cover the finished rice balls with a damp tea towel and set aside.

4 Lay a rice ball on a flat work area add a small dab of the wasabi paste (optional). Top the rice ball with a slice of eggplant. Repeat with remaining rice balls and eggplant. (Keep at room temperature – best if eaten within one hour.)

5 To serve, arrange the rice balls on a platter with a small lump of wasabi paste and a mound of sliced pickled ginger. Place a small bottle of soy sauce on the side.

Braised Shiitake Mushroom Sushi

Serves 4 to 6

1 cup	vegetable stock (p 7/8) or water	250 mL
½ lb	shiitake mushrooms, stems removed	250 g
1 Tb	light soy sauce	15 mL
1 Tb	garlic, minced	15 mL
2 Tb	dry sherry (or dry white wine)	30 mL
1 cup	cold water	250 mL
1 tsp	rice vinegar	5 mL
2 cups	cooked sushi rice (p 34)	500 mL
	Wasabi paste	
	Pickled ginger for garnish	
	Soy sauce	

1 In a small saucepan, combine stock, mushroom caps, light soy sauce, garlic and sherry. Bring to a boil over medium-high heat, then reduce the heat and simmer uncovered for 5 minutes. Remove from the heat and set aside to cool.

2 In a small bowl, combine water and rice vinegar. With clean hands, dip your fingers into the vinegar water and then scoop up a lump of sushi rice the size of a golf ball. Gently press into a compact ball and place on a platter. Repeat with the remaining rice, while continuing to dip your hands into the vinegar water and wiping them free of rice starch. Cover the finished rice balls with a damp tea towel and set aside.

3 Drain the mushrooms, reserving the broth as mushroom stock for another use. Lay a rice ball on a flat work area and add a small dab of wasabi paste (optional). Top the rice ball with a piece of the cooked mushroom. Repeat with the remaining rice balls and mushrooms. (Keep at room temperature – best if eaten within one hour.)

4 To serve, arrange the rice balls on a tray (wooden, if possible), with a small lump of wasabi paste and a mound of sliced pickled ginger. Place a small bottle of soy sauce on the side.

Use small whole shiitake mushrooms, or cut larger specimens into bite-size chunks. The sherry complements the rich caramel flavours of the mushroom and soy.

Charred Asparagus Roll, p 38
Country-style Sushi Salad, p 41

Spinach and Pickled Ginger Rolls

Serves 4 to 6

SUSHI MAYONNAISE

1 tsp	sesame oil	5 mL
2 Tb	sesame seeds	30 mL
¼ cup	low-fat mayonnaise (or tofu mayonnaise)	50 mL
2 Tb	pickled ginger, minced	30 mL
	Salt and pepper	

SPINACH AND PICKLED GINGER ROLLS

½ lb	spinach, stemmed	250 g
1 cup	cold water	250 mL
1 tsp	rice vinegar	5 mL
4 sheets	nori (seaweed)	4 sheets
2 cups	cooked sushi rice (p 34)	500 mL
	Wasabi paste	
	Pickled ginger for garnish	
	Soy sauce	

The combination of emerald green spinach and pink pickled ginger is vibrant and colourful. Sushi mayonnaise is a versatile condiment that works well with rice and is delicious in a tomato sandwich.

1 In a small bowl, combine sesame oil and seeds, mayonnaise and pickled ginger. Season well with salt and pepper, stirring to mix well. Set aside.

2 Bring a small stockpot filled with salted water to a boil. Add spinach and cook for 2 minutes. Quickly drain and transfer spinach to a bowl of ice water. Remove from the water when cool, and squeeze gently to remove as much water as possible. Set aside.

3 In another small bowl, combine water and rice vinegar. Lay the sheets of nori on a flat work area. With clean hands, dip your fingers into the vinegar water and scoop up a small handful of sushi rice. Place the sushi rice in the middle of the nori and spread out to an even thickness of ½ inch (1 cm). Repeat with additional rice until the nori is covered, except for a strip 1 inch (2.5 cm) wide along the top edge of the sheet. Keep dipping your hands in the vinegar water and wiping them free of rice starch.

4 Place ¼ of the spinach in a compact line across the bottom edge of the rice. Top with ¼ of the sushi mayonnaise. Fold the bottom of the nori sheet over the filling and roll up into a solid log. Dip your finger in the vinegar water and rub it on the empty part of the nori to seal the log with a smooth seam. Repeat with the remaining sheets of nori, rice, spinach and sushi mayonnaise.

5 To serve, use a sharp knife to slice the rolls into bite-size pieces. Arrange the slices on a platter, with a small lump of wasabi paste and a mound of sliced pickled ginger. Place a small bottle of soy sauce on the side.

Spinach Salad with Sautéed Mushrooms, Caramelized Shallots and Roasted Garlic Dressing, p 77

Potato, Corn and Rosemary Griddle Cakes, p 142

Charred Asparagus Roll

Serves 4 to 6

½ lb	asparagus, trimmed	250 g
1 Tb	garlic, minced	15 mL
1 Tb	olive oil	15 mL
	Salt and pepper	
4 sheets	nori (seaweed)	4 sheets
1 cup	cold water	250 mL
1 tsp	rice vinegar	5 mL
2 cups	cooked sushi rice (p 34)	500 mL
1 batch	sushi mayonnaise (p 37)	1 batch
	Wasabi paste	
	Pickled ginger for garnish	
	Soy sauce	

Choose young, slim stalks of asparagus for this dish. If only larger specimens are available, split the stalks lengthwise into halves or quarters, then proceed with the recipe. Charring the asparagus slightly on the outside brings out deep flavour while leaving the interior crisp and sweet.

1 In a shallow casserole dish, combine asparagus, garlic and olive oil. Season well with salt and pepper. Transfer to a nonstick skillet and sauté over medium-high heat for 3 to 4 minutes, stirring occasionally, until the asparagus begins to char. Remove from the heat and set aside. Let cool to room temperature.

2 In a small bowl, combine water and rice vinegar. Lay the sheets of nori on a flat work area. With clean hands, dip your fingers into the vinegar water and scoop up a small handful of sushi rice. Place the sushi rice in the middle of the nori and spread out to an even thickness of ½ inch (1 cm). Repeat with additional rice until the nori is covered, except for a strip 1 inch (2.5 cm) wide along the top edge of the sheet. Keep dipping your hands in the vinegar water and wiping them free of rice starch.

3 Place ¼ of the asparagus in a compact line across the bottom edge of the rice. Top with ¼ of the sushi mayonnaise. Fold the bottom of the nori sheet over the filling and roll up into a solid log. Dip your finger in the vinegar water and rub it on the empty part of the nori to seal the log with a smooth seam. Repeat with the remaining sheets of nori, rice, asparagus and mayonnaise.

4 To serve, use a sharp knife to slice the rolls into bite-size pieces. Arrange the slices on a platter, with a small lump of wasabi paste and a mound of sliced pickled ginger. Place a small bottle of soy sauce on the side.

Cucumber and Avocado Roll

Serves 4 to 6

1 cup	cold water	250 mL
1 tsp	rice vinegar	5 mL
4 sheets	nori (seaweed)	4 sheets
2 cups	cooked sushi rice (p 34)	500 mL
1	English cucumber, julienned	1
1	ripe avocado, julienned	1
1 batch	sushi mayonnaise (p 37)	1 batch
	Wasabi paste	
	Pickled ginger for garnish	
	Soy sauce	

1 In a small bowl, combine the water and rice vinegar. Lay the sheets of nori on a flat work area. With clean hands, dip your fingers into the vinegar water and scoop up a small handful of sushi rice. Place the sushi rice in the middle of the nori and spread out to an even thickness of ½ inch (1 cm). Repeat with additional rice until the nori is covered, except for a strip 1 inch (2.5 cm) wide along the top edge of the sheet. Keep dipping your hands in the vinegar water and wiping them free of rice starch.

2 Place ¼ of the cucumber and avocado strips in a compact line across the bottom edge of the rice. Top with ¼ of the sushi mayonnaise. Fold the bottom of the nori sheet over the filling and roll up into a solid log. Dip your finger in the vinegar water and rub it on the empty part of the nori to seal the log with a smooth seam. Repeat with the remaining sheets of nori, rice, cucumber, avocado and mayonnaise.

3 To serve, use a sharp knife to slice the rolls into bite-size pieces. Arrange the slices on a platter, with a small lump of wasabi paste and a mound of sliced pickled ginger. Place a small bottle of soy sauce on the side.

The contrast of crunchy cucumber and soft avocado is a sensual combination. Cut the avocado just before making the rolls. A drizzle of lemon juice will keep the avocado from turning brown if the dish must sit before serving.

Teriyaki Red Pepper and Baby Corn Cones

Makes 8 cones

TERIYAKI GLAZE

¼ cup	sweet soy sauce (p 18) or teriyaki sauce	50 mL
1 tsp	ginger, shredded	5 mL
1 tsp	hot sauce (or to taste)	5 mL
1 Tb	sake (optional)	15 mL

RED PEPPER AND BABY CORN CONES

1 Tb	vegetable oil	15 mL
1 cup	red peppers, seeded and julienned	250 mL
12	baby corn cobs (fresh, canned or frozen)	12
4 sheets	nori (seaweed)	4 sheets
1 cup	cold water	250 mL
1 tsp	rice vinegar	5 mL
2 cups	cooked sushi rice (p 34)	500 mL
	Wasabi paste	
	Pickled ginger for garnish	
	Soy sauce	

1 In a small bowl, combine sweet soy sauce, ginger, hot sauce and sake. Mix well and set aside.

2 In a nonstick skillet, heat vegetable oil. Add red peppers and baby corn cobs. Sauté over high heat for 4 to 5 minutes, or until tender and starting to brown. Add teriyaki glaze and toss to coat well. Remove from the heat and let cool.

3 Cut each nori sheet in half on a diagonal, to end up with a total of 8 triangles. In another small bowl, combine the water and rice vinegar. Lay the nori on a flat work area. With clean hands, dip your fingers into the vinegar water and scoop up a small handful of sushi rice. Place the sushi rice on a nori triangle and flatten into a long, cigar-shaped lump. Place a very thin coating of wasabi paste on top of the rice.

4 Place a few strips of red pepper and baby corn cobs alongside the rice. Fold one side of the nori triangle over the filling, trying to keep a sharp point at the bottom while rolling into a cone – the vegetable filling should stick out of the top of the cone. Dip your finger in the vinegar water and rub on the nori along the length of the cone to seal it with a smooth seam. Repeat with the remaining rice and fillings.

5 To serve, arrange the cones, seam side down, on a platter. Add a small lump of wasabi paste and a mound of sliced pickled ginger. Place a small bottle of soy sauce on the side.

A sushi cone should look something like an ice cream cone. Remember to wet the edge of the nori sheet and press it lightly to seal the cone. Place the cones seam side down on the serving plate.

Country-style Sushi Salad

Serves 6 to 8

1 Tb	vegetable oil	15 mL
1 Tb	garlic, minced	15 mL
1 cup	asparagus, sliced	250 mL
1 cup	red peppers, seeded and diced	250 mL
1 cup	zucchini, diced	250 mL
1 cup	snow peas, cut in half	250 mL
1 Tb	pickled ginger, minced	15 mL
1	green onion, sliced	1
4 cups	cooked sushi rice (p 34)	1 L
1 Tb	chives, minced	15 mL
2 Tb	sesame seeds	30 mL
	Pickled ginger for garnish	

1 In a nonstick skillet, heat vegetable oil. Add garlic, asparagus, red peppers, zucchini and snow peas. Sauté over medium-high heat for about 5 minutes, or until the asparagus turns bright green and softens. Add the pickled ginger and green onion, tossing to mix well.

2 Add the cooked sushi rice to the pan, tossing well to separate grains and distribute the vegetables. Remove from the heat and allow to sit for 5 minutes.

3 Serve warm or at room temperature. Transfer the rice mixture to bowls and garnish with chives and sesame seeds. Arrange a small mound of pickled ginger in the middle of each bowl. Place a small bottle of soy sauce on the side.

This dish may be served as an appetizer or as a main course. The rice can be made well in advance and reheated. Substitute any garden fresh vegetables for the ones in the recipe. Be sure to cut everything into evenly sized pieces.

Soups and Chowders

Asparagus and Spinach Soup with Herbed Goat's Cheese Quenelles

Serves 4

½ cup	goat's cheese	125 mL
2 Tb	mixed herbs, minced	30 mL
(chives, parsley, fennel, thyme, lovage, etc.)		
Freshly ground black pepper		

ASPARAGUS AND SPINACH SOUP

4 cups	vegetable stock (p 7/8)	1 L
1 lb	asparagus, trimmed and chopped	500 g
½ lb	spinach, stemmed and chopped	250 g
¼ cup	sour cream	50 mL
Salt and pepper to taste		
Chopped mixed herbs for garnish		

1 In a small bowl, combine goat's cheese, herbs and black pepper, mashing with a spoon or spatula to soften the cheese. Return to the fridge and allow to solidify for 20 minutes. Dip a tablespoon in hot water, then scoop out ¼ of the cheese mixture. With a second spoon, scoop the cheese from the first spoon, moulding the edges smooth. Gently place the quenelle on a clean plate. Repeat to make 3 more quenelles. Refrigerate until needed.

2 In a small stockpot, combine stock and asparagus, reserving asparagus tips. Bring stock to a boil and cook asparagus, uncovered, for 7 to 8 minutes, or until soft. Add spinach and cook for an additional 2 minutes. Transfer the soup to a blender or food processor and purée in batches (place a dish towel on top of the blender and press down firmly to avoid splashing the hot liquid).

3 Strain the soup through a coarse sieve, pressing solids with the back of a spoon or spatula, and return to the stove. Add the reserved asparagus tips and sour cream, then simmer, stirring constantly for 3 to 4 minutes, or until asparagus tips are tender. Season well with salt and pepper.

4 To serve, ladle the soup into bowls and top each at the last minute with a goat's cheese quenelle. The cheese will begin to melt and dissolve into the hot soup. Garnish with a sprinkling of chopped mixed herbs.

This *lovely, green-coloured soup is the perfect starter for an elegant spring meal. As the goat's cheese quenelles melt into the hot soup, they form a frothy topping and add a rich, delicate flavour.*

Hot and Sour Summer Vegetable Soup

Serves 4

4 cups	stock, vegetable (p 7/8) or mushroom (p 9/10)	1 L
1 cup	tomato juice	250 mL
2 Tb	garlic, minced	30 mL
1 Tb	ginger-citrus syrup (p 16), or liquid honey	15 mL
2	green onions, thinly sliced	2
1 cup	broccoli florets	250 mL
1 cup	corn kernels	250 mL
1	small zucchini, diced	1
1 cup	snow peas	250 mL
1 cup	tomatoes, diced	250 mL
2 tsp	hot sauce (or to taste)	10 mL
2 Tb	rice vinegar	30 mL
2 Tb	cilantro (or basil), minced	30 mL
	Salt and pepper to taste	
2 Tb	cornstarch (mixed with equal amount of water)	30 mL
	Chopped cilantro (or basil) for garnish	

1 In a small stockpot, combine stock, tomato juice, garlic and ginger-citrus syrup. Bring to a boil over high heat. Add green onions, broccoli, corn, zucchini, snow peas and tomatoes. Reduce the heat to medium and simmer uncovered for 6 to 7 minutes, or until the broccoli is tender.

2 Season the soup with hot sauce, rice vinegar, cilantro, salt and pepper. Bring the soup back to a rolling boil, whisking in the cornstarch mixture until the soup thickens.

3 To serve, ladle the soup into bowls and garnish with cilantro.

This soup is a quick one-pot summer meal. Try adding different fresh herbs, such as mint, lemon balm or rosemary. Or try a squeeze of fresh lime or lemon juice just before serving. Instead of garnishing with cilantro, try using a heaping pile of bean sprouts.

Tomato, Honey, Lemon and Basmati Rice Soup

Serves 4

Juice and zest of 1 lemon		
2 Tb	honey	30 mL
1 tsp	cinnamon	5 mL
2 cups	vegetable stock (p 7/8)	500 mL
2 cups	tomato juice	500 mL
½ cup	raw basmati rice	125 mL
2 Tb	garlic, minced	30 mL
Salt and pepper to taste		
Minced parsley (or cilantro) for garnish		

1 In a small stockpot, combine lemon zest and juice, honey, cinnamon, stock, tomato juice, raw rice and garlic. Bring to a boil, then reduce the heat and simmer uncovered for 15 to 20 minutes, or until rice is tender. Season with salt and pepper. Thin with additional stock if necessary.

2 To serve, ladle the soup into bowls and garnish with parsley.

This is a tangy spin on the classic comfort food of tomato soup. The honey-lemon mixture adds both acidity and sweetness. For a more substantial soup, add braising greens or spinach. Any leftover soup can be thickened with a little cornstarch and water for use as a sauce with polenta or tofu topped with vegetables.

Caribbean-spiced Black Bean Soup with Coconut Sour Cream

Serves 4 to 6

COCONUT SOUR CREAM

1 cup	sour cream	250 mL
½ cup	canned coconut milk	125 mL
Salt and pepper to taste		

BLACK BEAN SOUP

4 cups	stock, vegetable (p 7/8) or mushroom (p 9/10)	1 L
2 cups	cooked black beans	500 mL
1 tsp	ground allspice	5 mL
1 tsp	ground coriander	5 mL
1 tsp	curry paste (p 14) or powder (p 15)	5 mL
1 cup	yams, peeled and finely diced	250 mL
1 cup	onions, finely diced	250 mL
½ cup	celery, finely diced	125 mL
1 Tb	garlic, minced	15 mL
1	small jalapeño pepper, seeded and minced	1
Chopped cilantro for garnish		

1 In a small bowl, combine sour cream and coconut milk. Season well with salt and pepper. Set aside.

2 In a small stockpot, combine stock, cooked black beans, ground allspice, ground coriander and curry paste. Bring to a boil, then reduce the heat and simmer uncovered for 5 minutes. Transfer the soup to a blender or food processor and purée in batches (place a dish towel on top of the blender and press down firmly to avoid splashing the hot liquid).

3 Return the soup to the stove, adding more stock (if necessary) to thin soup. Bring to a boil, then reduce the heat and add yams, onions, celery, garlic and jalapeño. Simmer for 10 minutes, or until yam is tender.

4 To serve, ladle the soup into bowls, drizzle with coconut sour cream and sprinkle with cilantro.

The deep earthy flavour of the black bean purée is balanced by the rich tropical coconut cream. Instead of cilantro as a garnish, try using basil or chives.

Split-Pea Soup with Moroccan Spices and Pita Croutons

Serves 4 to 6

Oven at 350°F (180°C)

PITA CROUTONS

1	pita bread, cut in small cubes	1
1 Tb	olive oil	15 mL
1 tsp	garlic, minced	5 mL
	Salt and pepper to taste	

SPLIT-PEA SOUP
WITH MOROCCAN SPICES

6 cups	vegetable stock (p 7/8)	1.5 L
2 cups	raw split yellow peas	500 mL
1 cup	carrots, diced	250 mL
1 cup	onions, diced	250 mL
1 Tb	garlic, minced	15 mL
1	small jalapeño pepper, seeded and minced	1
1 tsp	ground coriander	5 mL
1 tsp	ground cumin	5 mL
1 tsp	cinnamon	5 mL
1 tsp	turmeric	5 mL
	Salt and pepper to taste	
	Chopped parsley for garnish	

1 In a small bowl, toss together pita bread, olive oil and garlic. Season with salt and pepper. Transfer to a baking sheet and toast in the oven for 5 minutes. Remove from the oven and set aside to cool.

2 In a small stockpot, combine stock, split peas, carrots, onions, garlic, jalapeño, coriander, cumin, cinnamon and turmeric. (NOTE: If your food processor has a plastic bowl, add the turmeric *after* processing the mixture and transferring it back to the stockpot, or else the turmeric will dye the plastic yellow.) Bring to a boil, then reduce the heat and simmer uncovered for 45 minutes, or until split peas are tender. Season with salt and pepper.

3 Transfer the soup to a blender or food processor and purée in batches (place a dish towel on top of the blender and press down firmly to avoid splashing the hot liquid).

4 Return the soup to the stockpot, adding more stock (if necessary) to thin. Bring to a boil, then reduce the heat and simmer uncovered for 20 minutes.

5 To serve, ladle the soup into bowls. Garnish with pita croutons and chopped parsley.

The exotic seasonings of North Africa spice up this smooth purée of yellow peas. The fragrant flavours of cinnamon and cumin perfume the kitchen as the soup cooks. For a more attractive presentation, slice the pita into thin ribbons and bake until crisp. Sprinkle the pita ribbons on top of the soup.

Chilled Tomato and Basil Soup with Sun-dried Tomato Salsa

Serves 4 to 6

Sun-dried Tomato Salsa

4 slices	sun-dried tomato slices	4 slices
1 cup	boiling water	250 mL
1 cup	tomato, diced	250 mL
1 tsp	garlic, minced	5 mL
¼ cup	onions, minced	50 mL
1 Tb	basil, minced	15 mL
1	small jalapeño pepper, seeded and minced	1
	Juice of 1 lime	
	Salt and pepper to taste	

Tomato and Basil Soup

4 cups	vegetable stock (p 7/8)	1 L
4 cups	tomatoes, diced	1 L
1 cup	zucchini, diced	250 mL
1 Tb	garlic, minced	15 mL
1 Tb	basil, minced	15 mL
	Salt and pepper to taste	
	Basil sprigs for garnish	

For a slightly richer salsa, add diced avocado. Before serving the soup, add a small splash of vodka or gin for a hint of sophistication.

1 In a small heatproof bowl, combine sun-dried tomato slices and boiling water. Let sit for 10 minutes, then remove tomato slices and dice finely. Return diced tomato to water and let sit for an additional 5 minutes.

2 In a small bowl, combine fresh tomato, garlic, onions, basil and jalapeño. Drain the sun-dried tomato and add to the fresh tomato mixture. Add lime juice, mixing well. Season salsa with salt and pepper and set aside.

3 In a medium saucepan, combine stock, tomatoes, zucchini and garlic. Bring to a boil, then reduce the heat and simmer uncovered for 10 minutes. Purée in a blender or food processor (place a dish towel on top of the blender and press down firmly to avoid splashing the hot liquid). Strain through a coarse sieve into a clean saucepan, pressing well with a spoon to release all the juices.

4 Return the soup to the heat and bring to a boil. Add basil and season well with salt and pepper. Reduce the heat and simmer uncovered for 5 minutes. Remove from the heat and let cool to room temperature. Transfer to a nonreactive bowl and chill in the refrigerator for at least 1 hour.

5 To serve, ladle the soup into bowls and top each with several large spoonfuls of salsa, mounded in the centre. Garnish with sprigs of basil.

Chilled Peach, Honey and Champagne Soup

Serves 4

2 cups	water (or peach cider)	500 mL
1 cup	dry white wine	250 mL
½ cup	honey	125 mL
½ tsp	pure vanilla extract	2 mL
6	peaches, pitted and halved	6
1 cup	champagne	250 mL
	Mint sprigs for garnish	

1. In a medium saucepan, combine water, white wine, honey and vanilla extract. Add peach halves and bring to a boil. Reduce the heat and simmer uncovered for 5 minutes. Remove from the heat and let sit for 20 minutes.

2. Remove the skin from the peaches and reserve the 4 best peach halves. Transfer the remaining cooking liquid and peach halves to a blender or food processor. Purée in batches until smooth. Transfer to a glass or ceramic bowl and let cool to room temperature. Place in the refrigerator and chill for at least 1 hour.

3. To serve, pour champagne into the soup, stirring gently. Ladle into chilled bowls (or large martini glasses). Place a poached peach half in each bowl and garnish with a mint sprig.

This soup makes an elegant starter for a celebratory meal. Use a fruity white wine such as Riesling or Chenin Blanc for the soup. A Chardonnay will also work, particularly when paired with a full-bodied champagne or blanc de blancs sparkling wine.

Sweet Corn and Barley Chowder with Chive Dumplings

Serves 4

CHIVE DUMPLINGS

2	eggs	2
½ cup	flour	125 mL
1 Tb	cornstarch	15 mL
¼ cup	chopped chives	50 mL
	Salt and pepper to taste	

CORN AND BARLEY CHOWDER

4 cups	stock, vegetable (p 7/8) or mushroom (p 9/10)	1 L
2 Tb	garlic, minced	30 mL
2 cups	corn kernels	500 mL
1 cup	cooked pearl barley	250 mL
1 cup	potatoes, peeled and diced	250 mL
½ cup	milk (or cream)	125 mL
	Salt and pepper to taste	
2 Tb	chives, chopped	30 mL

1   In a small bowl, whisk eggs. Add flour and cornstarch, whisking well to incorporate. Stir in chives and season with salt and pepper. Set aside.

2   In a small stockpot, combine stock, garlic, corn, cooked barley and potatoes. Bring to a boil, then reduce the heat and simmer uncovered for 5 minutes. Add milk and simmer uncovered for another 5 minutes. Season with salt and pepper.

3   Drop the dumpling mixture by the teaspoon (5 mL) into the simmering soup. Cook uncovered for about 10 minutes, or until the dumplings are firm.

4   To serve, ladle the soup into bowls and garnish with chives.

The barley offers an earthy, chewy counterpoint to the sweet corn. You can use frozen kernels, but fresh, in-season corn (particularly the variety called Peaches and Cream) makes the best soup. Instead of chives in the dumplings, try rosemary or sage.

Delicata Squash, Apple and Wild Rice Chowder

Serves 4

4 cups	stock, vegetable (p 7/8) or mushroom (p 9/10)	1 L
1 Tb	garlic, minced	15 mL
2 cups	delicata squash, peeled and diced	500 mL
1 cup	potatoes, peeled and diced	250 mL
1 cup	apples, peeled and diced	250 mL
1 Tb	sage, minced	15 mL
2 Tb	cornstarch (mixed with equal amount of water)	30 mL
2 cups	cooked wild rice (p 116)	500 mL
	Salt and pepper to taste	
	Parsley, chopped, for garnish	

1 In a small stockpot, combine stock, garlic, squash, potatoes, apples and sage. Bring to a boil, then reduce the heat and simmer uncovered for 15 minutes, or until the potatoes and squash are slightly tender.

2 Add cornstarch mixture, stirring until the soup thickens. Add cooked wild rice, then season with salt and pepper. Cook for 5 minutes.

3 To serve, ladle the soup into bowls and garnish with parsley.

Any type of winter squash, such as Japanese kabocha squash, acorn squash, banana squash or pumpkin, will work in this recipe. For the apples, use a firm variety like Fuji or Granny Smith.

Polish-style Chanterelle and Root Vegetable Chowder

Serves 4 to 6

2 Tb	olive oil (or melted butter)	30 mL
1 cup	onions, diced	250 mL
2 Tb	garlic, minced	30 mL
1 lb	chanterelles, sliced (or hedgehog, porcini, crimini, button, etc.)	500 g
1 cup	potatoes, peeled and diced	250 mL
1 cup	carrots, diced	250 mL
½ cup	celery, diced	125 mL
3 Tb	flour (or potato starch)	45 mL
2 cups	stock, mushroom (p 9/10) or vegetable (p 7/8)	500 mL
2 cups	milk	500 mL
2 Tb	lovage (or parsley or celery leaves), minced	30 mL
	Salt and pepper to taste	
	Minced lovage (or parsley or celery leaves) for garnish	

1 In a medium saucepan, heat olive oil. Add onions, garlic and chanterelles. Sauté over high heat for about 5 minutes, or until chanterelles are soft and appear dry. Reduce the heat to medium and add potatoes, carrots and celery. Continue to cook uncovered for 5 to 6 minutes.

2 Sprinkle flour over the vegetables, stirring to mix well. Cook for 2 to 3 minutes, then add stock, milk and lovage. Bring to a boil, then reduce the heat and simmer uncovered for 10 minutes, or until vegetables are tender. Season with salt and pepper.

3 To serve, ladle into bowls and garnish with lovage.

Mushrooms are a favourite in Polish cuisine. This hearty chowder is equally tasty with many other types of mushrooms, such as porcini, cep, button or shiitake.

Noodle Soups

Roast Garlic Broth with Rice Vermicelli, Spinach and Bean Sprouts

Serves 4

½ cup	garlic cloves from roasted garlic confit (p 13)	125 mL
4 cups	stock, vegetable (p 7/8) or mushroom (p 9/10)	1 L
1 cup	carrots, julienned	250 mL
½ lb	vermicelli rice noodles	250 g
2 cups	spinach (or young pea tops)	250 mL
	Salt and pepper to taste	
2 Tb	cilantro (or basil), chopped	30 mL
1 cup	bean sprouts	250 mL
	Sprigs of cilantro for garnish	

1 In a blender or food processor, combine roasted garlic confit and 1 cup (250 mL) of the stock. Purée until smooth. Transfer to a stockpot and add the remaining stock and carrots. Bring to a boil, then reduce heat and simmer uncovered for 5 minutes, or until carrots are tender. Set aside on low heat.

2 Meanwhile, place rice noodles in a heat-proof bowl and cover with boiling water. Let sit for 3 to 4 minutes, or until noodles are soft. Drain noodles and rinse with cold water.

3 Bring the soup to a boil. Add noodles (cut with scissors if small pieces are desired). Add spinach, stirring to mix well. Season with salt and pepper. Stir in cilantro.

4 To serve, ladle the soup into bowls. Garnish with the bean sprouts and a sprig of cilantro.

Instead of the vermicelli rice noodles, use bean thread (glass) noodles or a fine-strand pasta like angel hair or spaghettini.

Indonesian-style Curried Vegetable Soup with Rice Noodles

Serves 4

½ lb	thin flat rice noodles	250 g
1 cup	canned coconut milk	250 mL
1 Tb	garlic, minced	15 mL
1 Tb	ginger, minced	15 mL
1 Tb	curry paste (p 14)	15 mL
4 cups	vegetable stock (p 7/8)	1 L
1 cup	corn kernels	250 mL
1	red pepper, seeded and julienned	1
1 cup	bok choy, sliced (or broccoli florets)	250 mL
	Salt and pepper to taste	
2 Tb	cilantro (or basil), minced	30 mL
2	green onions, thinly sliced	2
2 Tb	cornstarch (mixed with equal amount of water)	30 mL
	Sprigs of cilantro for garnish	

1 Place rice noodles in a heatproof bowl and cover with boiling water. Let sit for 3 to 4 minutes, or until noodles are soft. Drain noodles and rinse with cold water. Set aside.

2 In a stockpot over medium-high heat, combine coconut milk, garlic, ginger and curry paste. Stir to mix well and cook for 1 to 2 minutes. Add stock and bring mixture to a boil, then reduce to a simmer. Add corn and red pepper, then continue cooking uncovered for 5 minutes, or until vegetables are tender.

3 Add noodles to the hot soup (cut with scissors if small pieces are desired). Add bok choy and season broth with salt and pepper. Add cilantro and green onions. Bring the soup to a boil and add cornstarch mixture, stirring until soup thickens.

4 To serve, ladle the soup into bowls and garnish with a sprig of cilantro.

Indonesian curries are typified by the use of coconut milk. For variety, try adding leeks, yellow zucchini, squash or parsnips to the broth.

Minestrone Soup with Braising Greens and Hazelnut Pesto

Serves 4

HAZELNUT PESTO

1 cup	hazelnuts	250 mL
1 cup	basil leaves	250 mL
1 Tb	garlic, minced	15 mL
½ cup	extra-virgin olive oil	125 mL
	Salt and pepper to taste	

MINESTRONE SOUP WITH BRAISING GREENS

4 cups	vegetable stock (p 7/8)	1 L
1 cup	tomato juice	250 mL
1 cup	dried small shell pasta (or macaroni)	250 mL
2 cups	braising greens, shredded (chard, kale, beet tops, mustard, etc.)	500 mL
1	green onion, minced	1
1 tsp	hot sauce (or to taste)	5 mL
	Salt and pepper to taste	

1 In a dry skillet, shaking the pan constantly, toast hazelnuts over medium-high heat for 4 to 5 minutes, or until nuts become fragrant and turn golden brown. Transfer to a clean kitchen towel and fold up the edges, then gather the towel and nuts into a ball. Rub the towel and nuts to remove any loose skins.

2 Transfer the nuts to a food processor, add basil and garlic, then pulse until a coarse paste is formed. Pour in olive oil in a slow steady stream until a smooth paste is formed. Season well with salt and pepper, then set aside.

3 In a stockpot, combine stock and tomato juice. Bring to a boil over medium-high heat and add pasta. Cook for 7 to 8 minutes, or until pasta is tender. Add braising greens and green onion. Season with hot sauce, salt and pepper. Reduce the heat and simmer for 2 to 3 minutes.

4 To serve, ladle the soup into bowls and top with a spoonful of hazelnut pesto.

This Italian-inspired soup can be made with a variety of other braising greens such as cabbage, Chinese greens or Japanese greens. If you are allergic (or not partial) to nuts, substitute toasted pumpkin or sunflower seeds for the hazelnuts in the pesto.

French Country Vegetable Soup with Egg Vermicelli

Serves 4 to 6

1 Tb	olive oil	15 mL
1 Tb	garlic, minced	15 mL
1 cup	onions, finely diced	250 mL
1 cup	mushrooms, diced	250 mL
½ cup	celery, finely diced	125 mL
1 cup	celeriac, diced	250 mL
1 cup	carrots, diced	250 mL
4 cups	stock, vegetable (p 7/8) or mushroom (p 9/10)	1 L
1 Tb	thyme, chopped	15 mL
1 Tb	marjoram, minced	15 mL
2 cups	fine egg vermicelli	500 mL
	Salt and pepper to taste	

1 In a stockpot, heat olive oil. Add garlic and onions. Sauté over medium-high heat for 5 minutes, or until onions soften and begin to brown. Add mushrooms, celery, celeriac and carrots. Continue cooking for 5 minutes, or until vegetables begin to brown.

2 Add stock, thyme and marjoram and bring to a boil, then reduce the heat and simmer uncovered for 10 minutes, or until vegetables are soft. Add vermicelli and continue to cook for about 5 minutes, or until pasta softens. Season with salt and pepper.

3 To serve, ladle soup into bowls.

This rustic soup is a hearty dish for a cool fall or winter evening. The egg vermicelli can be fresh or dried, and many types of fresh mushrooms such as porcini, button or chanterelle can be used.

Caramelized Onion Broth with Mushroom Won Tons

Serves 4

CARAMELIZED ONION BROTH

2 cups	caramelized onions (p 26)	500 mL
4 cups	mushroom stock (p 9/10)	1 L
1 Tb	sweet soy sauce (p 18)	15 mL

MUSHROOM WON TONS

1 Tb	olive oil	15 mL
1 cup	mushrooms, diced	250 mL
1 Tb	garlic, minced	15 mL
1 Tb	rosemary, minced	15 mL
	Salt and pepper to taste	
16	won ton wrappers	16
1	egg, beaten with 1 tsp/5 mL water	1

Frozen won ton wrappers are sold at many supermarkets and most Asian food stores. The clear, caramelized onion broth provides a delicate and refined base for the mushroom won tons. You can use any type of mushroom in the filling. Near the end of the cooking time, add a splash of sherry or Madeira for another layer of flavour. For an attractive presentation, garnish the soup with chopped chives or green onion.

1 In a medium saucepan, combine onions, stock and sweet soy sauce. Bring to a boil, then reduce the heat and simmer uncovered for 10 minutes. Remove from the heat and set aside.

2 In a nonstick skillet, heat olive oil. Add mushrooms, garlic and rosemary. Season well with salt and pepper. Sauté over medium-high heat for 5 minutes, or until the mushrooms start to brown and are fairly dry. Remove from the heat and allow to cool.

3 On a flat work area, place one won ton wrapper. Brush with egg wash and place 1 teaspoon (5 mL) of mushroom mixture in the middle of the wrapper. Pick up the corners of the wrapper and bring together over top of the filling. Squeeze gently and twist to make a firm seal. Set aside on a plate and repeat with remaining mushroom mixture and wrappers.

4 Bring the broth to a boil. Add the won tons and cook for 1 to 2 minutes, or until they float to the surface.

5 To serve, ladle the soup into bowls.

Mixed Asian Greens with Ramen Noodles in Spicy Soy-Basil Broth

Serves 4 to 6

4 cups	vegetable stock (p 7/8)	1 L
1 Tb	garlic, minced	15 mL
1 Tb	ginger, minced	15 mL
1 Tb	sweet soy sauce (p 18)	15 mL
½ lb	gai lan	250 g
1 cup	sui choy (or green cabbage), shredded	250 mL
8	baby bok choys	8
1 pkg	ramen noodles	1 pkg
1 tsp	hot sauce (or to taste)	5 mL
2 Tb	cilantro, chopped	30 mL
2 Tb	basil, chopped	30 mL
	Salt and pepper to taste	
1 tsp	sesame oil	5 mL
	Chopped cilantro (or basil) for garnish	

1 In a small stockpot, combine stock, garlic, ginger and sweet soy sauce. Bring to a boil, then reduce the heat and simmer uncovered for 2 to 3 minutes.

2 Add gai lan and cook for 2 to 3 minutes. Toss in sui choy, bok choys and ramen noodles. Return the soup to a boil and cook for 2 to 3 minutes, or until the noodles are soft. Add hot sauce, cilantro, basil, salt and pepper.

3 To serve, ladle into bowls. Drizzle with sesame oil and garnish with cilantro.

Ramen noodles, available fresh or dried, are handy for making quick meals. Gai lan, often called Chinese broccoli, has a crisp texture and a slightly bitter flavour. Many other types of Asian greens work well in the dish, especially Japanese ones like mitsuba, mizuna and tat soi. For a spicy anise flavour, add a tablespoon (15 mL) of shredded Thai basil.

Asian-spiced Root Vegetable Chowder over Thin Shanghai Noodles

Serves 4

4 cups	vegetable stock (p 7/8)	1 L
1 cup	carrots, cubed	250 mL
1 cup	yams, peeled and cubed	250 mL
1 cup	potatoes, peeled and cubed	250 mL
1 cup	parsnips, cubed	250 mL
2 pods	whole star anise	2 pods
1 Tb	ginger, minced	15 mL
2 Tb	dark soy sauce	30 mL
1 Tb	brown sugar	15 mL
2 Tb	cornstarch	30 mL
	(mixed with equal amount of water)	
1 tsp	sesame oil	5 mL
	Salt and pepper to taste	
1 lb	thin Shanghai noodles	500 g
	Vegetable oil	

1 In a small stockpot, combine stock, carrots, yams, potatoes, parsnips, star anise, ginger, dark soy sauce and brown sugar. Bring to a boil, then reduce the heat and simmer uncovered for 10 minutes, or until vegetables are tender.

2 Add cornstarch mixture, stirring until soup thickens. Season with sesame oil, salt and pepper. Use a slotted spoon to remove the whole star anise pods and discard. Set aside the soup on low heat.

3 Bring a stockpot filled with water to a boil. Add noodles, stirring well to distribute strands. Boil for 4 to 5 minutes, or until noodles are tender. Drain and coat with a little vegetable oil.

4 To serve, divide noodles among bowls and ladle soup over top.

Braising the root vegetables yields a thick, flavourful chowder. The Shanghai noodles can be replaced with fresh pasta like linguine or fettuccine. If you can't find whole star anise pods, use a scant 1 teaspoon (5 mL) of powdered star anise or five-spice powder.

Spaghettini in Black Bean Broth with Asparagus and Bean Sprouts

Serves 4

1 Tb	vegetable oil	15 mL
1 Tb	garlic, minced	15 mL
1 Tb	ginger, minced	15 mL
½ lb	asparagus, trimmed and cut into slices ¼"/5 mm thick	250 g
1 Tb	black bean sauce	15 mL
4 cups	stock, vegetable (p 7/8) or mushroom (p 9/10)	1 L
1 Tb	sweet soy sauce (p 18)	15 mL
1 tsp	hot sauce (or to taste)	5 mL
2 Tb	cornstarch (mixed with equal amount of water)	30 mL
	Salt to taste	
1 lb	dried spaghettini (or angel hair pasta)	500 g
1 cup	bean sprouts	250 mL
2 Tb	cilantro, chopped	30 mL
2	green onions, sliced	2

1 In a nonstick skillet, heat vegetable oil. Add garlic and ginger. Sauté over medium-high heat for about 1 minute, or until fragrant. Add asparagus and sauté for 2 to 3 minutes, or until softened.

2 Add black bean sauce and stir well to coat asparagus. Add stock, sweet soy sauce and hot sauce. Bring mixture to a boil, then reduce the heat to medium and simmer for 2 to 3 minutes. Add cornstarch mixture, stirring until soup thickens. Set aside the soup on low heat.

3 Bring a stockpot filled with salted water to a boil. Add the pasta, stirring well as it softens to distribute strands. Boil for 6 to 7 minutes, or until noodles are tender.

4 To serve, drain pasta and divide among bowls. Ladle soup over top. Garnish with bean sprouts, cilantro and green onions.

This dish is a combination of vegetables cloaked in an intense broth that uses fermented black beans, ginger and garlic. Instead of the asparagus and bean sprouts, try using cabbage, cauliflower and zucchini.

Roasted Eggplant–Tomato Soup with Orzo Pasta and Basil Sour Cream

Serves 4
Oven at 350°F (180°C)

Basil Sour Cream

1 cup	basil leaves	250 mL
1 Tb	extra-virgin olive oil	15 mL
1 cup	sour cream	250 mL
	Salt and pepper to taste	

Eggplant-Tomato Soup

4 cups	eggplant, peeled and diced	1 L
8	tomatoes, cut in half	8
16	garlic cloves, peeled	16
2 Tb	olive oil	30 mL
	Salt and pepper to taste	
4 cups	vegetable stock (p 7/8)	1 L
1 Tb	rosemary, minced	15 mL
1 Tb	thyme, minced	15 mL
1 cup	dried orzo pasta	250 mL
	Basil sprigs for garnish	

Roasting vegetables con-centrates the essence of summer into a soup bowl. Be sure to use extra-virgin olive oil for this dish, as it will shine through the sour cream and add a rich, sensual finish to the soup. You can serve this soup hot or cold. Pack it in a thermos bottle for a summertime picnic or outing.

1 In a blender or food processor, combine basil, extra-virgin olive oil and sour cream. Process until a smooth purée is formed. Season well with salt and pepper. Set aside.

2 In a roasting pan, combine eggplant, tomatoes and garlic cloves. Drizzle with olive oil and season well with salt and pepper. Place in a hot oven and roast for 30 minutes, or until vegetables are soft and beginning to brown.

3 Remove from the oven and allow to cool to room temperature. Transfer vegetables to a large saucepan. Pour a little boiling water into the roasting pan to deglaze and add to the saucepan.

4 To the saucepan, add stock, rosemary and thyme. Bring to a boil and simmer for 10 minutes. Remove from the heat and process in batches in a blender or food processor (cover with a kitchen towel to avoid splashing hot liquid).

5 Strain soup through a coarse sieve and return to the stove. Bring to a boil, add pasta and cook for 8 to 10 minutes, or until orzo is soft and the soup has slightly thick-ened. Season well with salt and pepper.

6 To serve, ladle the soup into bowls. Garnish with a dollop of basil sour cream and a sprig of basil.

Sweet Corn and Shiitake Mushroom Soup with Macaroni

Serves 4 to 6

1 Tb	vegetable oil	15 mL
1 cup	onions, diced	250 mL
2 Tb	garlic, minced	30 mL
1 cup	shiitake mushrooms, stemmed and sliced	250 mL
1 cup	corn kernels	250 mL
4 cups	stock, mushroom (p 9/10) or vegetable (p 7/8)	1 L
1 cup	dried macaroni pasta	250 mL
¼ cup	chives, chopped	50 mL
	Salt and pepper to taste	

1 In a medium saucepan, heat vegetable oil. Add onions and garlic. Sauté over medium-high heat for 5 minutes, or until the onions soften. Add mushrooms and continue to cook for 4 to 5 minutes, or until mushrooms are soft and appear dry.

2 Add corn, stock and macaroni. Bring mixture to a boil and cook for 7 to 8 minutes, or until pasta is tender. Add chives, then season well with salt and pepper.

3 To serve, ladle the soup into bowls.

This is a simple, quick soup that is a comforting combination of corn, mushrooms and pasta in a light broth. For a richer version, thicken the soup with 2 tablespoons (30 mL) of cornstarch mixed in an equal amount of water. Feel free to substitute button or oyster mushrooms for the shiitakes.

Green Salads

Romaine Salad with Mustard-Hoisin Dressing and Sesame Croutons

Serves 4
Oven at 350 °F (180 °C)

SESAME CROUTONS

2 Tb	vegetable oil	30 mL
1 tsp	sesame oil	5 mL
1 Tb	garlic, minced	15 mL
1 Tb	toasted sesame seeds	15 mL
2 cups	bread cubes	500 mL
	Salt and pepper to taste	

MUSTARD-HOISIN DRESSING

2 Tb	hoisin sauce	30 mL
1 Tb	mustard	15 mL
1 Tb	garlic, minced	15 mL
2 Tb	water	30 mL
1 Tb	apple cider vinegar	15 mL
¼ cup	vegetable oil	50 mL
	Salt and pepper to taste	

1 head	romaine lettuce	1 head

1　In a bowl, combine vegetable oil, sesame oil, garlic and sesame seeds. Add bread cubes, tossing to coat well. Season well with salt and pepper. Transfer to a baking sheet and toast in the oven for 10 minutes, or until bread begins to brown. Remove from the oven and set aside to cool.

2　In another bowl, mix together hoisin sauce, mustard, garlic, water and apple cider vinegar. Whisk in vegetable oil in a slow steady stream until a smooth emulsion is formed. Season well with salt and pepper. Set aside.

3　Tear lettuce leaves into bite-size pieces and place in a serving bowl. Add dressing and toss to coat well.

4　To serve, divide salad among plates and top with a healthy helping of sesame croutons.

Similar to a Caesar salad, this one is a crunchy blend of Sesame Croutons and crisp lettuce tossed in intensely flavoured Mustard-Hoisin Dressing. If you like a garlic kick in your salad, add as much as you and your guests can tolerate.

Sesame Strudel Stuffed with Mushrooms, Leeks and Greens, p 92

Lollo Rosso Salad with Zucchini and Carrots in Citrus-Miso Dressing

Serves 4

Citrus-Miso Dressing

2 Tb	miso	30 mL
2 Tb	hot water	30 mL
1 tsp	sesame oil	5 mL
1 Tb	garlic, minced	15 mL
2 Tb	ginger-citrus syrup (p 16) or liquid honey	30 mL
2 Tb	lemon juice	30 mL
	Freshly ground black pepper (or hot sauce) to taste	

Lollo Rosso Salad with Zucchini and Carrots

1	carrot, julienned	1
1	zucchini, seeded and julienned	1
1 head	lollo rosso lettuce	1 head
1	green onion, thinly sliced	1

1 In a bowl, combine miso, hot water, sesame oil, garlic, ginger-citrus syrup and lemon juice. Stir well to mix. If necessary, thin with additional hot water to form a smooth dressing. Season with freshly ground black pepper.

2 Add carrot and zucchini to dressing and toss to coat well. Let sit for at least 5 minutes to allow vegetables to absorb flavours.

3 To serve, tear lettuce leaves into bite-size pieces and divide among plates. Use a slotted spoon to remove the vegetables from the dressing and divide among the plates. Drizzle any remaining dressing over the salads. Garnish with a sprinkling of green onion.

Lollo rosso is a soft Italian lettuce (the name means "red leaf") that has green leaves with a ruffled border of crimson. Substitute any soft lettuce such as butter lettuce or oak leaf.

This salad keeps well, so it can be made in advance as a first course or as part of a buffet. Try adding bell peppers, celery or cucumber.

Chilled Carrot, Kaffir Lime and Ginger Custard with Green Curry Sauce, p 94

Heritage Tomato–Arugula Salad with Goat's Cheese Dressing

Serves 4

GOAT'S CHEESE DRESSING

¼ cup	soft goat's cheese	50 mL
2 Tb	hot water	30 mL
1 tsp	garlic, minced	5 mL
1 Tb	basil, minced	15 mL
2 Tb	white wine vinegar	30 mL
2 Tb	extra-virgin olive oil	30 mL
	Salt and pepper to taste	

TOMATO-ARUGULA SALAD

3 Tb	olive oil	45 mL
1	clove garlic, minced	1
1 Tb	minced basil	15 mL
	Salt and pepper to taste	
4 slices	sourdough bread	4 slices
4	heritage tomatoes, thinly sliced	4
1 cup	arugula leaves	250 mL
	Sprigs of basil	
	Toasted chopped hazelnuts for garnish (optional)	

1 In a small bowl, combine goat's cheese and hot water, using the back of a spoon to soften the cheese. Mix in garlic, basil, and white wine vinegar. Whisk in extra-virgin olive oil in a slow steady stream until a smooth emulsion is formed. Thin with additional water if necessary to make a smooth dressing. Season with salt and pepper. Set aside.

2 In another small bowl, combine olive oil, garlic and basil. Mix well, using the back of a spoon to lightly crush garlic into the oil. Season with salt and pepper.

3 Place bread slices on a plate and sprinkle with the oil and garlic mixture. Place a nonstick skillet over medium-high heat for 45 seconds. Add the bread and pan-fry for about 2 minutes, or until lightly browned. Flip the bread, then reduce the heat to medium and cook for 2 to 3 minutes, or until lightly browned. Transfer each bread slice to a warmed plate.

4 To serve, top each bread slice with ¼ of the arugula leaves. Place the tomato slices, slightly overlapping, on top of the arugula. Season with salt and pepper. Spoon a little of the goat's cheese dressing over tomatoes and garnish with a sprig of basil and hazelnuts (optional).

Heritage tomatoes come in many unusual flavours and colours. Try Old Flame, Orange Sunburst, Golden Pear or Red Currant tomatoes for a beautiful and exciting salad. Instead of basil in the dressing, try thyme or rosemary for an interesting variation. The Goat's Cheese Dressing is also a good topping for grilled vegetables like asparagus or green onions.

Mesclun Salad with Grilled Peppers and Green Beans in Soy-Honey Vinaigrette

Serves 4
Preheat barbecue or broiler

SOY-HONEY VINAIGRETTE

2 Tb	light soy sauce	30 mL
2 Tb	honey	30 mL
1 tsp	sesame oil	5 mL
1 Tb	garlic, minced	15 mL
2 Tb	rice vinegar	30 mL
¼ cup	vegetable oil	50 mL
	Salt and pepper to taste	

MESCLUN SALAD WITH GRILLED PEPPERS AND GREEN BEANS

2	red peppers, seeded and quartered	2
4 oz	green beans, trimmed	125 g
1 Tb	garlic, minced	15 mL
1 Tb	olive oil	15 mL
	Salt and pepper to taste	
½ lb	mesclun salad mix	250 g
	Toasted sesame seeds for garnish	

1 In a bowl, stir together light soy sauce, honey, sesame oil, garlic and rice vinegar. Whisk in vegetable oil in a slow steady stream until a smooth emulsion is formed. Season well with salt and pepper. Set aside.

2 In another bowl, combine red peppers, green beans, garlic and olive oil. Season well with salt and pepper. Transfer to a hot grill (or place on a baking sheet under a broiler) and cook for 7 to 8 minutes, or until the vegetables begin to char and soften. Transfer back to the bowl, pour soy-honey vinaigrette over top and cover with plastic wrap. Allow to cool to room temperature.

3 To serve, divide mesclun mix among plates. Use a slotted spoon to remove the grilled vegetables from the dressing and mound them on top of the greens. Drizzle the salads with the remaining vinaigrette. Garnish with sesame seeds.

Mesclun is a mixture of European and Asian greens that is often sold premixed in many food stores. You can make your own mesclun mix by combining small pieces of lettuce with radicchio, arugula and a Japanese green like mizuna or tat soi. The Soy-Honey Vinaigrette is a good all-purpose dressing for lettuce-based salads, as well as for coleslaw.

Mixed Greens, Tomato and Cucumber with Wasabi-Chive Vinaigrette

Serves 4

WASABI-CHIVE VINAIGRETTE

2 tsp	wasabi paste	10 mL
2 Tb	mustard	30 mL
2 Tb	ginger-citrus syrup (p 16) or liquid honey	30 mL
1 Tb	water	15 mL
2 Tb	rice vinegar	30 mL
¼ cup	vegetable oil	50 mL
1 Tb	pickled ginger, minced	15 mL
2 Tb	chives, finely chopped	30 mL
	Salt and pepper to taste	

MIXED GREENS, TOMATO AND CUCUMBER SALAD

1 head	lettuce	1 head
1 cup	arugula	250 mL
1 cup	radicchio, cored and shredded	250 mL
2 cups	Asian greens (mizuna, mitsuba, tat soi, mustard, etc.)	500 mL
1 cup	tomatoes, cubed	250 ml
1 cup	English cucumber, cubed	250 ml
¼ cup	pickled ginger	50 ml
	Chives for garnish	

1 In a bowl, stir together wasabi paste, mustard, ginger-citrus syrup, water and rice vinegar. Whisk in vegetable oil in a slow steady stream until a smooth emulsion is formed. Add the pickled ginger and chives. Season well with salt and pepper. Set aside.

2 Chop lettuce leaves into a coarse dice. In a salad bowl, combine lettuce, arugula, radicchio and Asian greens. Sprinkle with tomato and cucumber. Add dressing and toss to coat well.

3 To serve, divide salad among plates. Garnish with a clump of pickled ginger and chives.

The mixed greens can be whatever greens you find in the refrigerator, garden or local store. The Wasabi-Chive Vinaigrette can be made in quantity and kept on hand in the refrigerator for 1 to 2 weeks. Wasabi is an acquired taste for some people, so start with the recipe amount but feel free to add more to punch up the dressing.

Butter Lettuce, Pecan and Apple Salad with Mustard Dressing

Serves 4

MUSTARD DRESSING

2 Tb	grainy mustard	30 mL
1 tsp	garlic, minced	5 mL
1 Tb	water (or apple juice)	15 mL
2 Tb	apple cider vinegar	30 mL
1 Tb	sherry (optional)	15 mL
½ cup	vegetable oil	125 mL
	Salt and pepper to taste	

BUTTER LETTUCE, PECAN AND APPLE SALAD

1 cup	pecans	250 mL
2 heads	butter lettuce	2 heads
2	apples (Fuji or Granny Smith), cored and thinly sliced	2
Crumbled blue cheese for garnish (optional)		
Paprika for garnish		

1 In a bowl, stir together mustard, garlic, water, apple cider vinegar and sherry (optional). Whisk in vegetable oil in a slow steady stream until a smooth emulsion is formed. Season well with salt and pepper. Set aside.

2 In a dry nonstick skillet, toast pecans over medium-high heat, shaking pan constantly, for 4 to 5 minutes, or until the nuts become fragrant and begin to brown. Transfer to a plate and set aside to cool.

3 Arrange the largest lettuce leaves on plates, overlapping them. Mound the small leaves in the middle of each plate. Arrange apple slices on top of the lettuce. Drizzle with mustard dressing. Garnish with pecans and blue cheese (optional), then sprinkle lightly with paprika.

The soft texture of the butter lettuce is a delicious contrast to the crunchy nuts and apple. Toasting the nuts will crisp them and revive the flavour. For the crumbled blue cheese, use a good quality Stilton or Roquefort.

Shredded Lettuce, Yellow Bean and Sunflower Sprout Salad with Creamy Lemon Dressing

Serves 4

CREAMY LEMON DRESSING

½ cup	sunflower seeds (shelled)	125 mL
½ cup	water	125 mL
	Juice and zest of 1 lemon	
1 tsp	honey	5 mL
2 Tb	apple cider vinegar	30 mL
¼ cup	vegetable oil	50 mL
	Salt and pepper to taste	

LETTUCE, YELLOW BEAN AND SUNFLOWER SPROUT SALAD

½ lb	yellow beans	250 g
1 head	iceberg lettuce	1 head
2 Tb	parsley (or cilantro), chopped	30 mL
1 cup	sunflower (or bean) sprouts	250 mL

1 In a blender or food processor, combine sunflower seeds, water, lemon juice and zest, honey and apple cider vinegar. Mix well to blend. Pour in vegetable oil in a slow steady stream until a smooth emulsion is formed. Season well with salt and pepper. Set aside.

2 Bring a small stockpot filled with salted water to a boil. Add yellow beans and cook uncovered for 7 to 8 minutes, or until bright yellow and tender. Remove the beans from the water and plunge into a bowl of cold water and ice. When cool, remove the beans from the water and drain on a paper towel-lined plate.

3 Roll lettuce leaves into a log and cut into a fine shred. Place the shredded lettuce in a salad bowl. Add half of the dressing and toss to coat well. Season with salt and pepper.

4 To serve, divide lettuce among plates and top with the chilled yellow beans. Drizzle the remaining dressing over the beans. Garnish with parsley and a bundle of sunflower sprouts.

The creamy texture of the lemony dressing does not come from dairy products but from the puréed sunflower seeds in it. Either green or yellow beans will work well in the salad. Instead of sunflower or bean sprouts, substitute corn sprouts or soybean sprouts.

Mixed Greens with Feta Cheese, Spiced Pumpkin Seeds and Green Olive Vinaigrette

Serves 4

SPICED PUMPKIN SEEDS

½ cup	pumpkin seeds (shelled)	125 mL
1 tsp	cayenne pepper	5 mL
Salt and pepper to taste		

GREEN OLIVE VINAIGRETTE

¼ cup	pitted green olives	50 mL
1 Tb	honey	15 mL
1 Tb	Dijon mustard	15 mL
3 Tb	water	45 mL
1 Tb	white wine vinegar	15 mL
¼ cup	olive oil	50 mL
Freshly ground black pepper to taste		

MIXED GREENS WITH FETA CHEESE SALAD

1 head	lettuce	1 head
1 cup	radicchio, cored and shredded	250 mL
1 cup	frisée (curly endive)	250 mL
1 cup	feta cheese, diced	250 mL

1 In a dry nonstick skillet, combine pumpkin seeds, cayenne pepper, salt and pepper. Toast over medium-high heat, shaking pan constantly, for 2 to 3 minutes, or until they become fragrant and begin to brown. Transfer to a plate and set aside to cool.

2 In a blender or food processor, combine green olives, honey, mustard, water and white wine vinegar. Pulse to purée olives to a smooth paste. Pour in olive oil in a slow steady stream until a smooth emulsion is formed. Season well with black pepper. Set aside.

3 Chop the lettuce leaves into a coarse dice and place in a salad bowl. Add radicchio and frisée. Add vinaigrette and toss to coat well.

4 To serve, divide salad among plates. Garnish with a sprinkling of feta and spiced pumpkin seeds.

Pumpkin seeds contain a lot of oil, so be careful while toasting not to burn or char them. Do not add salt to the dressing, as the olives and feta cheese supply enough of it. To reduce the salt, rinse the olives and cheese before using.

Grilled Endive, Pear and Red Onions on Mesclun Greens with Balsamic Dressing

Serves 4
Preheat barbecue or broiler

4 heads	endive, split	4 heads
2	red Bartlett pears, cored and quartered	2
2	red onions, peeled and thickly sliced	2
1 Tb	garlic, minced	15 mL
3 Tb	extra-virgin olive oil	45 mL
3 Tb	balsamic vinegar	45 mL
	Salt and pepper to taste	
4 cups	mesclun mix	1 L

1   In a bowl, combine endive, pears, red onions, garlic, extra-virgin olive oil and balsamic vinegar. Season well with salt and pepper, then toss to coat well.

2   Use tongs to transfer vegetables (reserving dressing in bowl) to a hot grill, or place on a baking sheet under a broiler. Cook for about 5 minutes, or until pears and vegetables begin to char and soften. Transfer back to the dressing in the bowl and allow to cool.

3   To serve, divide mesclun mix among salad plates. Use tongs to transfer grilled onions, endive and pears to plates. Criss-cross each serving with two pieces of grilled endive and two pieces of grilled pear. Drizzle with the remaining dressing (adding more extra-virgin olive oil and balsamic vinegar if necessary).

Grilling the endive helps to eliminate a lot of the bitterness from the leaves. The balsamic vinegar adds a little sweetness and colour to the salad. Grill the pears lightly for the best results. Instead of Bartlett pears, you can use Bosc. For a richer salad, garnish with crumbled goat's cheese.

Spinach Salad with Sautéed Mushrooms, Caramelized Shallots and Roasted Garlic Dressing

Serves 4

ROASTED GARLIC DRESSING

½ cup	garlic cloves from roasted garlic confit (p 13)	125 mL
2 Tb	balsamic vinegar	30 mL
¼ cup	oil from roasted garlic confit	50 mL
	Salt and pepper to taste	

SPINACH SALAD WITH SAUTÉED MUSHROOMS AND CARAMELIZED SHALLOTS

1 lb	spinach leaves, stemmed	500 g
1 Tb	olive oil	15 mL
1 cup	shallots, peeled and sliced	250 mL
1 Tb	garlic, minced	15 mL
	Salt and pepper to taste	
1 tsp	honey	5 mL
½ lb	mushrooms, stemmed and sliced (shiitake, crimini, oyster, portobello)	250 g
	Grated Parmesan cheese for garnish (optional)	

1 In a blender or food processor, combine roasted garlic cloves, balsamic vinegar and water. Pulse until mixture forms a smooth purée. Pour in oil from roasted garlic confit in a slow steady stream until a smooth emulsion is formed. Season well with salt and pepper. Set aside.

2 Place spinach in a salad bowl and set aside.

3 In a nonstick skillet, heat olive oil. Add shallots and garlic, then season well with salt and pepper. Sauté over medium-high heat for 5 minutes, or until shallots soften. Add honey, stirring well to dissolve. Allow honey to caramelize with shallots for 2 to 3 minutes. Add mushrooms and sauté for 4 to 5 minutes, or until they are soft and appear dry.

4 Add the hot mushroom mixture to the spinach. Add the dressing and toss to coat well.

5 To serve, divide salad among plates. Garnish with a sprinkling of Parmesan.

The heat of the warm mushrooms, shallots and garlic will wilt the spinach a bit. For the mushrooms, use a blend of wild and cultivated types; in the spring, I add a few fresh morels.

Vegetable Salads

Shredded Sui Choy, Carrot and Bean Sprout Salad with Allspice Honey-Mustard Dressing

Serves 4

ALLSPICE HONEY-MUSTARD DRESSING

1 tsp	ground allspice (or cloves)	5 mL
2 Tb	Dijon (or any other) mustard	30 mL
1 Tb	liquid honey	15 mL
1 Tb	apple cider vinegar	15 mL
1 Tb	water (or apple juice)	15 mL
¼ cup	vegetable oil	50 mL
	Salt and pepper to taste	

SUI CHOY, CARROT AND BEAN SPROUT SALAD

4 cups	sui choy, cut in thin strips	1 L
2 cups	carrots, grated	500 mL
2 cups	bean (or corn or sunflower) sprouts	500 mL
	Salt and pepper to taste	
2 Tb	cilantro, chopped	30 mL

1   In a bowl, stir together allspice, mustard, honey, apple cider vinegar and water. Whisk in vegetable oil in a slow steady stream until a smooth emulsion is formed. Season well with salt and pepper. Set aside.

2   In a salad bowl, combine sui choy, carrots and bean sprouts. Add dressing and toss to coat well. Season with salt and pepper.

3   To serve, divide salad among plates and garnish with cilantro.

Allspice and mustard help to brighten and add interest to the dressing. Instead of the allspice, cloves would work well as a foil to the juicy flavours of the sui choy and carrots. If this salad is left to sit for too long, juices will be drawn from the vegetables and the dressing will become watery. For best results, serve within 30 minutes of adding the dressing to the salad.

Balsamic-roasted Beet Salad with Hazelnut Sour Cream Dressing

Serves 4
Oven at 350°F (180°C)

BALSAMIC-ROASTED BEETS

4	medium whole beets	4
2 Tb	olive oil	30 mL
	Salt and pepper to taste	
2 Tb	balsamic vinegar	30 mL

HAZELNUT SOUR CREAM DRESSING

1 Tb	Frangelico liqueur (or any nut liqueur)	15 mL
1 cup	sour cream	250 mL
1 Tb	hazelnut or olive oil (optional)	15 mL
	Salt and pepper to taste	
1 cup	hazelnuts, toasted, skinned and coarsely chopped	250 mL
	Curly endive (or other salad green) for garnish	

1 Wash beets and place in a colander to dry for 5 minutes. Transfer to a roasting pan and drizzle with olive oil, using your hands to rub the oil all over the beets. Season well with salt and pepper. Roast in the oven for 45 minutes, or until a knife easily pierces the beets. Remove from the oven and allow to cool to handling temperature, then remove skin from the beets. Cut beets into thin slices and place in a bowl. Drizzle with balsamic vinegar and set aside.

2 In another bowl, combine liqueur and sour cream. Whisk in hazelnut oil in a slow steady stream until a smooth emulsion is formed. Season well with salt and pepper. Set aside.

3 To serve, overlap the beet slices to form a circle in the middle of each plate. Place a large dollop of sour cream dressing in the centre of each beet circle. Scatter hazelnuts around the edge of the plates and on top of the salad. Stick a sprig of curly endive into each mound of sour cream.

Roasting beets with their skin on brings out a whole other dimension of flavour. Instead of hazelnuts and Frangelico in the dressing, substitute your favourite nut and its matching liqueur: almond with amaretto, or walnut with nocino.

Mushrooms and Shallots Marinated in Sweet Soy, Cilantro and Sesame

Serves 4 to 6

SWEET SOY, CILANTRO AND SESAME MARINADE

2 cups	rice vinegar	500 mL
¼ cup	sweet soy sauce (p 18)	50 mL
1 Tb	ginger, minced	15 mL
1 Tb	garlic, minced	15 mL
2 Tb	cilantro, chopped	30 mL
1 tsp	sesame oil	5 mL
1 tsp	hot sauce (or to taste)	5 mL

½ lb	shallots, peeled	250 g
1 lb	mushrooms, cut in bite-size pieces (shiitake, oyster, chanterelle or button)	500 g
1 Tb	toasted sesame seeds	15 mL
	Cilantro for garnish	

1 In a nonreactive saucepan, combine rice vinegar, sweet soy sauce, ginger, garlic, cilantro, sesame oil and hot sauce. Bring to a boil over medium-high heat.

2 Add shallots, then reduce the heat and simmer uncovered for 5 minutes. Add mushrooms and continue to simmer, stirring occasionally, for another 5 minutes. Remove from the heat.

3 To serve, transfer mixture to a glass or ceramic serving dish and cool to room temperature. Garnish with sesame seeds and sprigs of cilantro.

Marinated mushrooms *are popular for appetizers and buffets. This dish can be made ahead, placed in a covered glass jar and refrigerated; it will keep for several days. Dense mushrooms, like chanterelles, are particularly good prepared this way. For a simple twist on this recipe, add 2 heaping tablespoonfuls (30 mL plus) of mustard to make a tasty mustard pickle.*

Honey-pickled Vegetables with Herbs, Spices and Apple Cider

Serves 4

HONEY PICKLING LIQUID

2 cups	apple cider vinegar	500 mL
2 cups	apple cider (or water)	500 mL
¼ cup	honey	50 mL
2 Tb	pickling spice	30 mL
5	whole cloves	5
1 Tb	rosemary, chopped	15 mL
1 Tb	sage, chopped	15 mL
1 Tb	thyme, chopped	15 mL
2 Tb	coarse salt	30 mL

1 cup	cauliflower florets	250 mL
1 cup	carrot sticks	250 mL
1 cup	zucchini sticks	250 mL
1 cup	baby corn cobs (fresh, canned or frozen)	250 mL

1 In a nonreactive saucepan, combine apple cider vinegar, apple cider, honey, pickling spice, cloves, rosemary, sage, thyme and salt. Bring to a boil over medium-high heat. Add cauliflower, carrots, zucchini and baby corn cobs, then reduce the heat and simmer uncovered for 5 minutes.

2 Remove from the heat and place on a cooling rack. Let cool to room temperature.

3 To serve, transfer pickled vegetables to a glass or ceramic bowl.

Inspired by traditional English pickles, this salad keeps well and is excellent for summer picnics. You can add other vegetables such as zucchini, mushrooms and peppers.

Shredded Carrot, Cucumber and Pickled Ginger Salad with Citrus Dressing

Serves 4

CITRUS DRESSING

Juice and zest of 1 lemon		
Juice and zest of 1 lime		
1 Tb	pickled ginger juice (or sake)	15 mL
2 tsp	wasabi paste (or dry mustard)	10 mL
¼ cup	vegetable oil	50 mL
Salt and pepper to taste		

CARROT, CUCUMBER AND PICKLED GINGER SALAD

4 cups	carrots, shredded	1 L
2 cups	cucumber, seeded and julienned	500 mL
½ cup	pickled ginger, shredded	125 mL
Shredded nori (seaweed) for garnish		

1 In a bowl, stir together lemon and lime juice, zests, pickled ginger juice and wasabi paste. Whisk in vegetable oil in a slow steady stream until a smooth emulsion is formed. Season well with salt and pepper. Set aside.

2 In a salad bowl, combine carrots, cucumber and pickled ginger. Add dressing and toss to coat well.

3 To serve, divide salad among plates and garnish with shredded nori.

This *Citrus Dressing is reminiscent of Japanese ponzu sauce (made from the juice of a citrus fruit). The tart bite of the dressing is balanced by the sweet crunch of the carrots.*

Green and Yellow Bean Salad with Thai Curry Dressing

Serves 4

THAI CURRY DRESSING

¼ cup	canned coconut milk	50 mL
1 cup	mango (or papaya), peeled and diced	250 mL
1 tsp	curry paste (p 14)	5 mL
1 Tb	ginger, minced	15 mL
1 Tb	garlic, minced	15 mL
	Juice and zest of 1 lime	
	Salt and pepper to taste	

GREEN AND YELLOW BEAN SALAD

½ lb	green beans, trimmed	250 g
½ lb	yellow beans, trimmed	250 g
1 cup	dry-roasted peanuts, chopped	250 mL
	Thai basil (or cilantro) for garnish	

1 In a blender or food processor, combine coconut milk, mango, curry paste, ginger, garlic, lime juice and zest. Pulse until a smooth mixture is obtained. Season well with salt and pepper. Set aside.

2 Fill a small stockpot with salted water and bring to a boil over high heat. Add the green and yellow beans, and cook uncovered for 8 to 10 minutes, or until bright in colour and tender. Remove the beans from the water and plunge into a bowl of cold water and ice. When cool, remove from the water and drain.

3 Place the cooked beans (reserving 4 of each colour) in a bowl. Add the dressing and toss to coat well.

4 To serve, divide beans among salad plates. Top each with one green and one yellow bean crossed. Garnish with peanuts and Thai basil.

The rich Thai Curry

Dressing, based on puréed mango and coconut milk, wraps the green and yellows beans in the intense flavours of Asia. This dish makes a beautiful starter for elegant entertaining.

Green Cabbage, Carrot and Daikon Coleslaw with Creamy Sesame Dressing

Serves 4

CREAMY SESAME DRESSING

½ cup	soft tofu	125 mL
2 Tb	miso	30 mL
1 tsp	sesame oil	5 mL
1 Tb	garlic	15 mL
2 Tb	rice vinegar	30 mL
¼ cup	vegetable oil	50 mL
	Salt and pepper to taste	

CABBAGE, CARROT AND DAIKON COLESLAW

4 cups	green cabbage, shredded	1 L
2 cups	carrots, shredded	500 mL
1 cup	daikon radish, shredded	250 mL
	Salt and pepper to taste	
2 Tb	toasted sesame seeds	30 mL

1. In a blender or food processor, combine tofu, miso, sesame oil, garlic and rice vinegar. Pulse until a smooth mixture is formed. Add vegetable oil in a slow steady stream until a smooth emulsion is formed. Season well with salt and pepper. Set aside.

2. In a bowl, combine cabbage, carrots and daikon radish. Season well with salt and pepper. Add dressing and toss to coat well.

3. To serve, divide among salad plates and garnish with sesame seeds.

The creamy texture of this Asian-style dressing comes from tofu, not dairy products. The mild radish taste of the daikon, the crunchy carrot and cabbage, and the rich sesame dressing make this a flavourful and satisfying salad.

Sweet and Sour Wild Rice Salad with Leeks, Mushrooms and Toasted Pine Nuts

Serves 4

SWEET AND SOUR DRESSING

1 cup	tomato juice	250 mL
1 Tb	maple syrup (or honey)	15 mL
2 Tb	lemon juice	30 mL
1 Tb	char sui (or barbecue) sauce	15 mL
1 tsp	hot sauce (or to taste)	5 mL

WILD RICE SALAD WITH LEEKS, MUSHROOMS AND TOASTED PINE NUTS

2 Tb	vegetable oil	30 mL
2 cups	leeks, chopped	500 mL
2 Tb	garlic, minced	30 mL
2 cups	mushrooms, cut in bite-size pieces	500 mL
	Salt and pepper to taste	
2 cups	cooked wild rice (p 116)	500 mL
1 cup	golden raisins (soaked in boiling water)	250 mL
½ cup	toasted pine nuts	125 mL
	Parsley, chopped for garnish	

1 In a nonreactive saucepan, combine tomato juice, maple syrup, lemon juice, char sui sauce and hot sauce. Bring to a boil over medium-high heat, then reduce heat and simmer uncovered for 5 minutes. Remove from the heat and allow to cool to room temperature.

2 In a nonstick skillet, heat vegetable oil. Add leeks, garlic and mushrooms. Season well with salt and pepper. Sauté over medium-high heat for 10 minutes, or until the mushrooms are soft and appear dry. Remove from the heat and allow to cool.

3 In a bowl, combine cooked wild rice, mushroom mixture and drained raisins. Add dressing and toss to coat well.

4 To serve, divide among salad plates. Top with a sprinkling of pine nuts and garnish with parsley.

The Sweet and Sour

Dressing is enhanced with char sui sauce, which is traditionally used for Chinese barbecue. If it is not available, substitute your favourite barbecue sauce. Instead of the pine nuts, you can use sliced almonds.

Cucumber, Red Pepper and Feta Cheese Salad with Honey-Lime Vinaigrette

Serves 4

HONEY-LIME VINAIGRETTE

	Juice and minced zest of 2 limes	
2 Tb	liquid honey	30 mL
2 Tb	mustard	30 mL
1 Tb	water	15 mL
¼ cup	vegetable oil	50 mL
	Salt and pepper to taste	

CUCUMBER, RED PEPPER AND FETA CHEESE SALAD

3 cups	English cucumber, diced	750 mL
1 cup	red peppers, seeded and diced	250 mL
1 cup	feta cheese, diced	250 mL
½ cup	pitted whole green olives (optional)	125 mL
2 Tb	chopped parsley (or cilantro)	30 mL

1 In a bowl, stir together lime juice, zest, honey, mustard and water. Whisk in vegetable oil in a slow steady stream until a smooth emulsion is formed. Season well with salt and pepper. Set aside.

2 In another bowl, combine cucumber, red peppers and feta cheese. Add dressing and toss to coat well.

3 To serve, divide among salad plates. Garnish with olives (optional) and parsley.

This simple summer salad is bound together by the bright Honey-Lime Vinaigrette. This dressing is also good with simple green salads or a rice noodle and vegetable salad. If you have access to imported kaffir lime from Thailand, add 1 minced leaf or a teaspoon (5 mL) of the fruit's zest to the dressing for an explosion of tropical flavour.

New Potato Nuggets with Lemon, Caper and Blackcurrant Dressing

Serves 4

2 lbs	new potato nuggets	1 kg
	LEMON, CAPER AND BLACKCURRANT DRESSING	
2 Tb	Dijon mustard	30 mL
	Juice and zest of 1 lemon	
1 Tb	capers, minced	15 mL
1 Tb	maple syrup (or liquid honey)	15 mL
2 Tb	extra-virgin olive oil	30 mL
	Salt and pepper	
1 cup	dried blackcurrants (soaked in boiling water)	250 mL
	Parsley, chopped, for garnish	

1 Bring a large saucepan filled with salted water to a boil. Add potatoes and cook uncovered for 8 to 10 minutes, or until tender. Drain and let cool to room temperature. Cut into halves or quarters and set aside.

2 In a bowl, stir together mustard, lemon juice and zest, capers and maple syrup. Whisk in extra-virgin olive oil in a slow steady stream until a smooth emulsion is formed. Season with salt and pepper. Add the potatoes and drained blackcurrants. Toss to coat well.

3 To serve, divide among salad plates and garnish with parsley.

The flavours of Sicily inspired the Lemon, Caper and Blackcurrant Dressing. In place of the blackcurrants, use your favourite variety of raisin – but be sure to rinse and soak them in boiling water to rehydrate. The potatoes are not peeled, as the delicate skin is very nutritious and helps to keep the flesh firm.

Tapas and Flatbreads

Sesame Strudel Stuffed with Mushrooms, Leeks and Greens

Serves 4 to 6
Oven at 400°F (200°C)

MUSHROOM, LEEK AND GREENS FILLING

1 Tb	vegetable oil	15 mL
1 Tb	garlic, minced	15 mL
1 Tb	ginger, minced	15 mL
1 cup	leeks, sliced	250 mL
½ lb	mushrooms, sliced	250 g
2 cups	braising greens (kale, arugula, Chinese greens)	500 mL
	Salt and pepper to taste	

SESAME STRUDEL

3 sheets	store-bought phyllo pastry	3 sheets
2 Tb	vegetable oil	30 mL
1 tsp	sesame oil	5 mL
¼ cup	sesame seeds	50 mL
2 cups	tomato sauce (p 11)	500 mL

Frozen phyllo pastry is sold at most supermarkets. It is a handy way to duplicate the crunch and flavour of traditional pastry at a fraction of the fat content. For a richer dish, place a little goat's cheese or mozzarella on top of the filling before rolling up the strudel.

1 In a nonstick skillet, heat vegetable oil. Add garlic and ginger. Sauté over medium-high heat for about 1 minute, or until fragrant. Add leeks and sauté for 3 to 4 minutes, or until they soften and begin to brown. Add mushrooms and sauté for about 5 minutes, or until they are soft and appear dry. Add braising greens and allow to wilt for 1 to 2 minutes. Season with salt and pepper. Remove from the heat and transfer to a colander (set over a bowl). Let cool to room temperature.

2 Lay one sheet of phyllo pastry on a flat work surface. Place the remaining sheets under a damp kitchen towel. In a small bowl, mix together vegetable and sesame oils. Brush a little mixed oil over the surface of the phyllo sheet and sprinkle evenly with ½ of the sesame seeds. Add the second sheet of phyllo, brush with the mixed oils and sprinkle with the remaining sesame seeds. Top with the third phyllo sheet. Transfer the layered phyllo to a baking sheet.

3 Place the filling in a compact strip near the bottom edge of the phyllo. Fold the bottom edge of the phyllo over the filling, mould into a log, then roll up into a tight cylinder. Brush the top edge with a little oil and press lightly to seal. (At this point, it can be refrigerated for 2 to 3 hours. Brush with oil to prevent drying.)

4 Brush the top of the strudel with oil and place, seam side down, on a baking sheet. Bake in the oven for 15 minutes, or until golden brown and crispy. While the strudel is baking, place tomato sauce in a small saucepan over medium heat and warm through.

5 To serve, use a serrated knife to cut the strudel into slices 2 inches (5 cm) thick. Place warm tomato sauce on heated plates and top with a slice of strudel.

Maple, Mustard and Balsamic Vinegar–glazed Asparagus

Serves 4

MAPLE, MUSTARD AND BALSAMIC VINEGAR GLAZE

2 Tb	mustard	30 mL
1 Tb	maple syrup (or liquid honey)	15 mL
2 Tb	balsamic vinegar	30 mL
1 tsp	hot sauce (or to taste)	5 mL
1 Tb	vegetable oil	15 mL
1 lb	asparagus, trimmed and halved	500 g
1 Tb	garlic, minced	15 mL
	Salt and pepper to taste	
½ cup	vegetable stock (p 7/8)	125 mL
1 Tb	toasted sesame seeds	15 mL

1 In a small bowl, stir together mustard, maple syrup, balsamic vinegar and hot sauce. Set the glaze aside.

2 In a nonstick skillet, heat vegetable oil. Add bottom halves of asparagus spears (cut thick pieces in half lengthwise) and sauté over medium-high heat for 3 to 4 minutes, or until beginning to brown. Add the asparagus tips and garlic. Season with salt and pepper. Sauté for 2 to 3 minutes.

3 Add stock to the asparagus mixture and increase the heat to high. Cook uncovered for about 5 minutes, or until all the liquid is evaporated and the asparagus is tender. Add the glaze and cook for 1 to 2 minutes, allowing it to thicken. Remove the pan from the heat.

4 To serve, arrange asparagus on a platter and garnish with a sprinkling of sesame seeds.

Pan-roasting asparagus concentrates the flavour and slightly chars the outside of the vegetable. The glaze is added near the end of cooking, as the sugar will burn quickly in a hot pan.

Chilled Carrot, Kaffir Lime and Ginger Custard with Green Curry Sauce

Serves 4
Oven at 325°F (160°C)

Carrot, Kaffir Lime and Ginger Custard

2 cups	vegetable stock (p 7/8) or water	500 mL
2 cups	carrots, sliced	500 mL
1	kaffir lime leaf (or zest of 1 lime)	1
1 Tb	ginger, minced	15 mL
2	whole eggs (or 3 egg whites)	2
½ cup	yogurt (or sour cream)	125 mL
	Salt and pepper to taste	

Green Curry Sauce

1 Tb	vegetable oil	15 mL
1 Tb	garlic, minced	15 mL
1 cup	onions, diced	250 mL
2 tsp	curry paste (p 14)	10 mL
1 cup	vegetable stock (p 7/8) or water	250 mL
1 cup	spinach leaves	250 mL
	Salt and pepper to taste	
	Small spinach leaves for garnish	

The orange-coloured carrot custard is placed in a spicy green pool of sauce. This striking dish takes a little effort and patience but results in a sophisticated starter for a special dinner. To unmould the custards more easily, dip a paring knife into hot water and run the blade inside the edge of the ramekins.

1 In a saucepan, combine stock, carrots, kaffir lime leaf and ginger. Bring to a boil, then reduce the heat and simmer for 15 minutes, or until the carrots are soft. Remove from the heat and allow to cool.

2 Use a slotted spoon to transfer carrots to a blender or food processor, reserving liquid. Discard kaffir lime leaf. While blending, add liquid slowly until smooth. Transfer to a small bowl, then whisk in eggs and yogurt. Season well with salt and pepper.

3 Spoon the carrot mixture into 4 lightly oiled individual custard dishes and place in a shallow roasting pan. Fill the pan with boiling water to ½ the height of the custard dishes. Cover the pan with foil and bake in the oven for 30 minutes, or until custard is just set. Remove from the oven and place on a cooling rack. Remove the custard dishes from the water when possible and let cool to room temperature. Chill in the refrigerator for at least 30 minutes before serving.

4 In a saucepan, heat vegetable oil. Add garlic and onions. Sauté over medium-high heat for 3 to 4 minutes, or until soft and beginning to brown. Add curry paste, stirring well to coat, and cook for 2 to 3 minutes, or until fragrant. Pour in stock and bring to a boil. Toss in the spinach, stirring, for about 1 minute, or until it wilts and turns deep green. Transfer to a blender or food processor and purée. Add more liquid if necessary to form a light sauce. Season with salt and pepper. Set aside.

5 To serve, run a sharp knife around the rim of one custard dish. With a quick motion, flip the custard dish upside-down over a plate, allowing the custard to slide out (tap gently to coax it out). Repeat with the remaining custards. Pour the curry sauce around each custard and garnish with spinach leaves.

Grilled Asian Vegetables with Black Bean Sauce

Serves 4
Preheat barbecue

BLACK BEAN SAUCE

1 Tb	vegetable oil	15 mL
1 tsp	ginger, minced	5 mL
1 tsp	garlic, minced	5 mL
2 Tb	black bean sauce	30 mL
4 cups	stock, vegetable (p 7/8) or mushroom (p 9/10)	1 L
1 tsp	hot sauce (or to taste)	5 mL
1 Tb	cornstarch (mixed with equal amount of water)	15 mL

GRILLED ASIAN VEGETABLES

½ lb	gai lan (Chinese broccoli) stems, trimmed	250 g
8	small bok choys, halved	8
2 cups	Japanese eggplant, cut in thick slices	500 mL
2 cups	zucchini, cut in thick slices	500 mL
2 Tb	olive (or vegetable) oil	30 mL
1 Tb	garlic, minced	15 mL
	Salt and pepper to taste	
	Chopped cilantro (or basil) for garnish	

1 In a saucepan, heat vegetable oil. Add ginger and garlic. Sauté over medium-high heat for about 1 minute, or until fragrant. Stir in black bean sauce, stock and hot sauce, then bring to a boil. Add cornstarch mixture, stirring constantly until the sauce thickens. Set aside and keep warm.

2 In a bowl, combine gai lan, bok choys, eggplant and zucchini. Add olive oil and garlic. Season well with salt and pepper. Toss to coat well. Place vegetables on the hot grill and cook for 3 to 4 minutes on each side, or until tender and slightly charred. Return to the bowl and keep warm.

3 To serve, arrange vegetables on a platter and pour warm sauce over top. Garnish with cilantro.

Asian vegetables are tasty, nutritious and usually cook very quickly. You can substitute more common vegetables like pepper, asparagus and eggplant with very good results.

Warm Lentils and Roasted Root Vegetables with Dijon-Chardonnay Vinaigrette

Serves 4 to 6
Oven at 400°F (200°C)

LENTILS AND ROASTED ROOT VEGETABLES

2 cups	French (Dupuy) lentils	500 mL
1 cup	potatoes, peeled and diced	250 mL
1 cup	carrots, diced	250 mL
1 cup	onions, diced	250 mL
1 cup	parsnips (or celeriac), diced	250 mL
1 Tb	garlic, minced	15 mL
2 Tb	olive oil	30 mL
	Salt and pepper to taste	

DIJON-CHARDONNAY VINAIGRETTE

½ cup	Chardonnay (or any dry white wine)	125 mL
2 Tb	Dijon mustard	30 mL
2 Tb	white wine vinegar	30 mL
1 tsp	honey	5 mL
¼ cup	vegetable oil	50 mL
1 tsp	garlic, minced	5 mL
	Salt and pepper to taste	
	Chopped parsley for garnish	

1　In a saucepan, combine lentils and 4 cups (1 L) water. Bring to a boil, then reduce the heat and simmer uncovered for 40 minutes, or until lentils are tender. Add more water if lentils appear dry. Remove from the heat and drain in a colander.

2　Meanwhile, in a roasting pan, combine potatoes, carrots, onions, parsnips, garlic and olive oil. Season well with salt and pepper and toss to mix. Roast in the oven for 20 minutes, stir well, then roast for another 10 minutes, or until the vegetables are soft and golden brown. Remove from the oven and let cool.

3　In a second saucepan, bring Chardonnay to a boil and reduce to half of its original volume. Pour into a bowl and stir in mustard, white wine vinegar and honey. Whisk in vegetable oil in a slow steady stream, or until an emulsion is formed. Stir in garlic and season with salt and pepper. Add lentils and roasted vegetables, tossing to coat well. Let rest for at least 15 minutes before serving.

4　To serve, transfer to a large bowl and garnish with chopped parsley.

Dupuy lentils are the highest quality available. They are deep olive green, with a firm texture and thin skin. If they are not available, use olive green or brown lentils (red lentils are too soft for this dish). This dish is best served at room temperature.

Sautéed Mixed Greens with Hazelnuts and Lemon-Thyme Vinaigrette

Serves 4

LEMON-THYME VINAIGRETTE

2 Tb	Dijon mustard	30 mL
1 tsp	garlic, minced	5 mL
1 Tb	lemon thyme (or any thyme), minced	15 mL
2 Tb	white wine vinegar	30 mL
1 Tb	water	15 mL
2 Tb	vegetable oil	30 mL
	Salt and pepper to taste	

SAUTÉED MIXED GREENS WITH HAZELNUTS

2 Tb	olive oil	30 mL
1 Tb	garlic, minced	15 mL
1 cup	arugula	250 mL
1 cup	mustard greens	250 mL
2 cups	kale, shredded	500 mL
1 cup	dandelion greens (or spinach)	250 mL
1 head	radicchio, cored and chopped	1 head
¼ cup	hazelnuts, toasted and chopped (p 58) (or chopped tomato or green onions)	50 mL

1 In a small bowl, stir together mustard, garlic, lemon thyme, white wine vinegar and water. Whisk in vegetable oil in a slow steady stream until an emulsion is formed. Season with salt and pepper. Set aside.

2 In a wok (or nonstick skillet), heat olive oil. Add garlic and sauté over medium-high heat for about 1 minute, or until fragrant. Add arugula, mustard greens, kale, dandelion greens and radicchio, then sauté for about 2 minutes, or until barely wilted. Add vinaigrette and toss to coat well.

3 To serve, arrange in a large bowl and garnish with chopped hazelnuts.

If lemon thyme is not available for the vinaigrette, substitute regular thyme together with a little lemon zest. This dish works well with many other herbs. For tasty variations, substitute fresh sage, rosemary or marjoram for the lemon thyme in the dressing.

Ginger-sautéed Spinach with Miso and Sunflower Seed Pesto

Serves 4

MISO AND SUNFLOWER SEED PESTO

2 Tb	miso	30 mL
1 Tb	garlic, minced	15 mL
½ cup	sunflower seeds (shelled)	125 mL
2 Tb	apple juice (or water)	30 mL
¼ cup	vegetable stock (p 7/8) or water	50 mL
	Salt and pepper to taste	

GINGER-SAUTÉED SPINACH

1 Tb	vegetable oil	15 mL
1 Tb	ginger, minced	15 mL
1 lb	spinach (or pea tops)	500 g
	Toasted shelled sunflower seeds for garnish	

1 In blender or food processor, combine miso, garlic, sunflower seeds and apple juice. Pulse to form a coarse paste. Add stock in a slow steady stream until a smooth paste is formed. Season with salt and pepper. Transfer to a small bowl and set aside.

2 In a wok or nonstick skillet, heat vegetable oil. Add ginger and sauté over medium-high heat for about 1 minute, until fragrant. Add spinach and sauté for about 2 minutes, or until barely wilted. Add pesto and toss to coat well.

3 To serve, transfer the spinach to a large bowl and garnish with sunflower seeds.

Spinach is excellent in this dish, but do try fresh pea tops from an Asian market or your garden. Pea tops are the young leaves and tendrils of the common snow pea. Two versions are available. The tender young shoots (with a translucent stem) are delicate and must be cooked very quickly. The more mature shoots are cooked like spinach.

Cauliflower, Green Onion and Asiago Cheese Griddle Cakes

Serves 4
Oven at 200°F (100°C)

2 cups	cauliflower florets	500 mL
2	whole eggs (or 4 egg whites)	2
¼ cup	flour	50 mL
2 tsp	baking powder	10 mL
1 tsp	salt	5 mL
1 tsp	cayenne pepper	5 mL
½ cup	green onions, sliced	125 mL
1 cup	Asiago cheese (or cheddar), grated	250 mL
1 Tb	olive oil	15 mL

1 Place cauliflower in a large saucepan filled with salted water and bring to a boil. Cook uncovered for 7 to 8 minutes, or until tender. Drain and let cool slightly. Place cauliflower and eggs in a blender or food processor. Pulse until a smooth mixture is formed. Set aside.

2 In a bowl, combine flour, baking powder, salt and cayenne pepper. Add the cauliflower purée. Stir in green onions and Asiago cheese until a fairly smooth batter is formed.

3 Pour olive oil into a nonstick skillet, then wipe pan with a paper towel (reserve it for further use). Place the skillet over medium-high heat. Drop 4 small griddle cakes, each about ¼ cup (50 mL), into the skillet and cook for 4 to 5 minutes per side (reduce the heat if browning too quickly). Transfer to a plate and keep warm in the oven. Repeat with the remaining batter, first rubbing the pan with the oiled paper towel each time.

4 To serve, remove the warm griddle cakes from oven and arrange on a platter.

These delicate griddle cakes may be served as an appetizer or a side dish. They can be made in advance and kept in a warm oven until needed, for up to 30 minutes. For a variation, try using puréed broccoli or yam instead of the cauliflower. White or orange cheddar may be used instead of the Asiago.

Mozzarella-Basil Cornbread with Tomatoes and Olives

Serves 4 to 6
Oven at 400°F (200°C)

1 cup	basil	250 mL
2 Tb	olive oil	30 mL
1 Tb	garlic, minced	15 mL
1 tsp	salt	5 mL
1 ½ cups	cornmeal	375 mL
1 cup	flour	250 mL
1 Tb	baking powder	15 mL
1 tsp	salt (second amount)	5 mL
2 Tb	brown sugar	30 mL
1	egg	1
1¾ cups	buttermilk	425 mL
1 cup	cherry tomatoes (or tomatoes, chopped)	250 mL
½ cup	pitted green olives, chopped	125 mL
1 cup	mozzarella cheese, grated	250 mL

1. In a blender or food processor, combine basil, olive oil, garlic and salt. Pulse until a smooth paste is formed (adding a little additional oil if necessary). Set aside.

2. In a bowl, stir together cornmeal, flour, baking powder, salt (second amount) and brown sugar. Add egg and buttermilk to the centre of the bowl, stirring to combine well (add a little more buttermilk if too dry). Fold in the basil purée and mozzarella until blended.

3. Pour batter into an oiled cast-iron skillet (or casserole dish) and top with tomatoes. olives and mozzarella. Bake in the oven for 30 minutes, or until a knife inserted in the centre comes out clean.

4. To serve, cut into squares (or wedges), and arrange on a platter.

The puréed basil gives the bread both flavour and an attractive green hue. The cast-iron skillet helps to form a nice crunchy crust on the bottom of the bread and also makes a rustic serving dish to bring to the table. For extra crunch, dust the oiled skillet with cornmeal before adding the batter.

Flatbread Topped with Thai-flavoured Spinach and Mushrooms

Serves 4
Oven at 200°F (100°C)

FLATBREAD DOUGH

¼-oz pkg	instant yeast	8-g pkg
3 cups	bread flour	750 mL
1 Tb	salt	15 mL
1 cup	warm water (more if needed)	250 mL
2 Tb	olive oil	30 mL

SPINACH AND MUSHROOM TOPPING

¼ cup	canned coconut milk	50 mL
1 Tb	ginger, minced	15 mL
1 tsp	curry paste (p 14)	5 mL
1 cup	shiitake mushrooms, chopped	250 mL
½ lb	spinach, stemmed	250 g
1 Tb	Thai basil (or basil), chopped	15 mL
	Additional olive oil	
1 Tb	toasted sesame seeds	15 mL

Instead of making the flatbread, you can buy premade pizza shells or focaccia.

1   In a food processor, combine yeast, flour and salt. Add warm water and olive oil in a slow steady stream, or until the dough comes together in a ball. Place on a floured work surface and knead for a few minutes, or until a smooth dough is formed. Transfer to an oiled bowl and cover with plastic wrap or a clean kitchen towel. Let sit for 60 to 90 minutes until double in size (or place in the refrigerator overnight).

2   On a flat work surface, lightly covered with flour, roll out ¼ of the dough and quickly knead into a smooth round. Repeat with remaining dough. Cover the rounds with a towel and allow to rest for 20 minutes. Use a rolling pin to roll out each round into a circle ½ inch (1 cm) thick and 8 inches (20 cm) across. Repeat with remaining dough to form 4 rounds.

3   In a nonstick skillet, combine coconut milk, ginger and curry paste. Cook over medium-high heat for 2 to 3 minutes to blend flavours. Add mushrooms, spinach and Thai basil. Toss well to coat and let the spinach wilt. Remove from the heat and set aside.

4   Heat a cast-iron pan over medium heat for 1 minute. Brush both sides of each flatbread with olive oil. Place one round in the hot pan and grill each side for 3 to 4 minutes, or until crisp and brown. Remove from the heat, top with ¼ of the spinach and mushroom mixture, then sprinkle with sesame seeds. Place in the oven to keep warm. Repeat process with remaining rounds of flatbread, spinach and mushroom mixture, and sesame seeds.

Corn, Shiitake Mushroom and Goat's Cheese Quiche with Savoury Rice Crust, p 121

Pizza with Herbs, Caramelized Onions, New Potatoes and Three Cheeses

Serves 2 to 4
Oven at 350°F (180°C)

1 recipe	flatbread dough (p 101)	1 recipe
12	small new potatoes	12
1 Tb	olive oil	15 mL
1	large onion, sliced	1
	Salt and pepper to taste	
1 Tb	sage, minced	15 mL
1 Tb	thyme, minced	15 mL
1 tsp	honey	5 mL
¼ cup	dry white wine	50 mL
2 Tb	semolina (or cornmeal)	30 mL
1 Tb	olive oil (second amount)	15 mL
	Salt and pepper to taste	
2 Tb	Parmesan cheese, grated	30 mL
½ cup	Asiago cheese, shredded	125 mL
½ cup	Swiss cheese, shredded	125 mL

This pizza was inspired by the traditional tarte flambée served in the Alsatian region of France. For the best results, use a pizza stone or perforated pizza pan dusted with flour. Once the pizza is out of the oven, sprinkle it with minced chives and parsley to brighten the flavour and appearance.

1 Make bread dough according to the recipe, up to the end of step one. When the dough has risen, place it on a lightly floured work surface, knead lightly, then roll into a single smooth ball. Cover with a towel and allow to rest for 20 minutes.

2 In the meantime, bring a saucepan filled with water to a boil. Add the potatoes and cook uncovered for 10 to 12 minutes, or until tender. Remove from the heat, drain and let cool. Cut potatoes into thin slices and set aside.

3 In a nonstick skillet, heat 1 tablespoon (15 mL) olive oil. Add onion and sauté over medium-high heat for 2 to 3 minutes, or until soft and beginning to brown. Season with salt and pepper. Add sage, thyme, honey and white wine, continuing to cook until the wine evaporates and onions are golden brown. Remove from the heat and set aside.

4 Roll out pizza dough into a circle the size of a 12-inch (30-cm) pizza pan. Sprinkle the pizza pan with semolina. Place dough on the pan, pressing out to cover the entire pan. Allow to rest for 5 minutes, then brush with olive oil (second amount). Sprinkle onion mixture over top and cover with potato slices. Season well with salt and pepper. Sprinkle with Parmesan, Asiago and Swiss cheese. Bake in the oven for 20 minutes, or until bottom is browned and cheese is beginning to colour. Remove from the oven and allow to rest for 2 to 3 minutes.

5 To serve, cut into wedges.

Noodles and Pasta

Crispy Chow Mein Cake Topped with Asparagus and Mushroom Cream

Serves 4

Oven at 400°F (200°C)

CHOW MEIN CAKE

1 lb	fresh chow mein noodles	500 g
4	green onions, sliced	4
1 tsp	sesame oil	5 mL
2 Tb	vegetable oil	30 mL
	Salt and pepper to taste	

ASPARAGUS AND MUSHROOM CREAM

1 Tb	ground dried mushrooms (p 10), (porcini, morel, shiitake, button, etc.)	15 mL
1 cup	whipping cream	250 mL
	Salt and pepper to taste	
1 Tb	vegetable oil	15 mL
1 Tb	garlic, minced	15 mL
1 cup	small button mushrooms, quartered	250 mL
1 lb	asparagus, in 1″ (2.5 cm) pieces	500 g
1 Tb	light soy sauce	15 mL
	Chopped parsley for garnish	

Baking the noodle cake produces a crisp nest for the asparagus and mushroom cream. The ground dried mushrooms infuse the cream sauce with a deep, rich mushroom flavour.

1 Place chow mein noodles in a heatproof bowl and cover with boiling water. Let sit for 2 to 3 minutes to soften. Drain well and shake to remove excess water. Wipe bowl dry, then return noodles and add green onions, sesame and vegetable oils. Season with salt and pepper and toss well.

2 In a dry, nonstick skillet, pan-fry the noodle mixture over medium-high heat, shaking pan occasionally, for 5 minutes, or until the bottom is crispy and brown. Flip the noodle cake onto a baking sheet and fluff it to give a bit of height. Bake in the oven for 15 minutes, or until crispy and browned. Turn off the oven but keep the noodle cake inside it to keep warm.

3 In a saucepan, combine ground dried mushrooms and cream. Season lightly with salt and pepper. Bring just to a boil over medium-high heat (watching carefully as the cream expands greatly). Immediately remove from the heat and set aside to cool.

4 In another nonstick skillet, heat vegetable oil. Add garlic, mushrooms and asparagus. Season well with salt and pepper. Sauté over medium-high heat for 5 minutes, or until the asparagus is tender and starting to brown. Add mushroom cream and light soy sauce. Reduce the heat to low and simmer uncovered for 3 to 4 minutes, or until the sauce thickens.

5 To serve, place the noodle cake on a platter and top with the asparagus and mushroom cream. Garnish with a sprinkling of parsley.

Udon Noodles with Soy-roasted Tomato and Corn Ragout

Serves 4
Oven at 375°F (190°C)

1 lb	Roma tomatoes, halved	500 g
1 Tb	garlic, minced	15 mL
2 Tb	olive oil	30 mL
	Freshly ground black pepper	
2 Tb	sweet soy sauce (p 18)	30 mL
1 cup	tomato juice	250 mL
3 cups	vegetable stock (p 7/8)	750 mL
1 tsp	hot sauce (or to taste)	5 mL
1 cup	red onions, cubed	250 mL
1 cup	corn kernels	250 mL
4	baby bok choys, quartered	4
1 Tb	cornstarch (mixed with equal amount of water)	15 mL
1 pkg	precooked udon noodles	1 pkg
	Chopped basil (or parsley) for garnish	

1 In a roasting pan, combine tomatoes, garlic and olive oil. Season well with black pepper and drizzle sweet soy sauce over top. Toss to mix well and roast in the oven for 20 minutes, or until tomatoes are soft and beginning to wrinkle and brown. Remove from the heat and let cool. Remove the tomato skins and discard.

2 Scrape the contents of the roasting pan into a stockpot. Pour tomato juice into the roasting pan and deglaze. Add to the stockpot along with stock, hot sauce, red onions, corn and baby bok choys. Bring to a boil, then reduce the heat and simmer uncovered for 5 to 6 minutes, or until the vegetables are tender. Add cornstarch mixture, stirring to thicken. Add udon noodles, tossing to coat well. Heat mixture for 2 to 3 minutes, or until noodles are warmed through.

3 To serve, use tongs to divide the mixture among bowls. Use a spoon to scoop up and divide the sauce. Garnish with a sprinkling of basil.

Japanese udon noodles are a thick, chewy, wheat-based noodle that is often made with exotic flours like yam and taro root. Chop the udon into bite-size pieces before cooking to make them more manageable for eating. Udon noodles are usually sold precooked and vacuum-packed.

Singapore-style Rice Noodles with Shredded Vegetables

Serves 4

½ lb	thin rice noodles (or vermicelli)	250 g
1 tsp	sesame oil	5 mL
2 Tb	vegetable oil	30 mL
1 Tb	ginger, minced	15 mL
1 cup	carrots, shredded	250 mL
1 cup	onions, thinly sliced	250 mL
1	red pepper, seeded and thinly sliced	1
	Salt and pepper to taste	
1 Tb	curry paste (p 14)	15 mL
¼ cup	vegetable stock (p 7/8) or water	50 mL
2 cups	bean sprouts	500 mL
	Chopped cilantro (or green onions) for garnish	

1 Place rice noodles in a heatproof bowl and cover with boiling water. Let sit for 2 to 3 minutes, or until the noodles are soft. Drain and shake off excess water. Toss with sesame oil and set aside.

2 In a nonstick skillet, heat vegetable oil. Add ginger, carrots, onions and red pepper. Season well with salt and pepper. Sauté over medium-high heat for 2 to 3 minutes, or until the vegetables are just tender. Add the curry paste and toss to coat well. Cook for about 2 minutes, or until fragrant.

3 Add stock to the vegetable mixture and bring to a boil, then reduce the heat and simmer uncovered for 3 to 4 minutes, or until the liquid is reduced by half. Add rice noodles and toss to coat well. The noodles will soften immediately and absorb the curry. Add the bean sprouts and toss to mix well.

4 To serve, transfer to a platter and garnish with cilantro.

Rice noodles usually have a pronounced stale flavour that disappears when they are properly soaked in boiling water. If they are not available, use fettuccine. For a tangy flavour boost, chop a few sweet pickles (or Chinese sweet and sour mustard greens) and stir them into the vegetables.

Thick Rice Noodles with Sweet and Sour Cauliflower Sauce

Serves 4

2 cups	cauliflower florets	500 mL
1 Tb	vegetable oil	15 mL
1 Tb	ginger, minced	15 mL
1 Tb	garlic, minced	15 mL
2 cups	tomato juice	500 mL
1 Tb	char sui (or hoisin) sauce	15 mL
1 Tb	honey	15 mL
2 Tb	rice vinegar	30 mL
1 Tb	cornstarch (mixed with equal amount of water)	15 mL
1 lb	fresh thick rice noodles (chow fun)	500 g
1	tomato, chopped for garnish	1

1 Bring a stockpot filled with salted water to a boil. Add cauliflower and cook for 4 to 5 minutes, or until tender. Strain into a colander, cool with cold running water and drain. Set aside.

2 In a nonstick skillet, heat vegetable oil. Add ginger and garlic. Sauté over medium-high heat for about 1 minute, or until fragrant. Add tomato juice, char sui sauce, honey and rice vinegar. Stir well to mix and bring to a boil. Add cornstarch mixture, stirring to thicken (if necessary thin with water).

3 Reduce the heat to medium and add cauliflower and rice noodles, tossing to coat well. The noodles will soften immediately and absorb the sauce. When the noodles are heated through, transfer to a platter and garnish with chopped tomato.

Thick rice noodles are sold fresh in many Asian markets. They are the best choice for this dish and worth the search. But if you cannot find them, substitute fettuccine. Instead of the cauliflower, try using eggplant, broccoli or mushrooms – or Asian greens such as bok choy, gai lan or sui choy.

Shanghai Noodles with Banana Squash and Apple Curry

Serves 4

1 Tb	vegetable oil	15 mL
1 Tb	ginger, minced	15 mL
1 Tb	garlic, minced	15 mL
2 cups	banana (or acorn) squash, peeled and julienned	500 mL
	Salt and pepper to taste	
1 Tb	curry paste (p 14)	15 mL
1 Tb	hoisin sauce	15 mL
2 cups	apple juice (or water)	500 mL
1 cup	apples, peeled and julienned	250 mL
1 cup	sui choy, shredded	250 mL
1 Tb	cornstarch (mixed with equal amount of water)	15 mL
	Juice of 1 lime	
1 lb	fresh thin Shanghai noodles	500 g
2 Tb	cilantro (or green onion), chopped	30 mL

1 In a wok (or large nonstick skillet), heat vegetable oil. Add ginger and garlic. Sauté over medium-high heat for about 1 minute, or until fragrant. Add squash and season well with salt and pepper. Sauté for 5 minutes, or until squash is tender and beginning to brown.

2 Add curry paste, hoisin sauce and apple juice to squash mixture, stirring well to dissolve. Add apples and sui choy. Bring to a boil, then add cornstarch mixture, stirring to thicken. Add lime juice and stir well to mix. Remove from the heat and keep warm.

3 Bring a stockpot filled with salted water to a boil. Add noodles and cook for 2 to 3 minutes, or until tender. Drain noodles in a colander and shake well to remove excess water.

4 To serve, transfer the noodles to a platter (or large bowl). Add sauce and toss to coat well. Garnish with cilantro.

Shanghai-style noodles are made from wheat flour in a variety of thicknesses. Banana squash, which has a sweet, delicate flavour, can reach gigantic proportions. It is usually sold cut into large chunks and wrapped in cellophane. When the squash is cut into a fine julienne, it cooks very quickly and has a fresh, delicate flavour.

Spinach Fettuccine with Spring Vegetable and Morel Ragout

Serves 4

1 cup	fiddlehead ferns (or asparagus)	250 mL
2 Tb	olive oil	30 mL
4	shallots, minced	4
1 Tb	garlic, minced	15 mL
	Salt and pepper to taste	
1 cup	new potatoes, quartered	250 mL
1 cup	morel mushrooms, sliced (or 12 dried morels, rehydrated)	250 mL
1 cup	asparagus, trimmed and sliced	250 mL
1 Tb	flour	15 mL
2 cups	vegetable stock (p 7/8)	500 mL
1 lb	fresh spinach fettuccine	500 g
1 Tb	olive oil (second amount)	15 mL
2 cups	spinach, stemmed	500 mL
¼ cup	sour cream (optional)	50 mL
2 Tb	chopped chives	30 mL

This dish is a true springtime creation that features the seasonal flavours and textures of new potatoes, asparagus, fiddleheads, spinach and morels. The sour cream helps to bind the flavours together but can be replaced by soy yogurt.

1 Before using fresh fiddleheads, they must be cooked in two changes of water. Place fiddleheads in a pot and cover with cold water. Bring to a boil and drain. Repeat process. (Frozen fiddleheads are sold in many supermarkets; follow the cooking directions on the package.)

2 In a nonstick skillet, heat 2 tablespoons (30 mL) olive oil. Add shallots and garlic. Season well with salt and pepper. Sauté over medium-high heat for about 1 minute, or until fragrant. Add fiddleheads, new potatoes, morels and asparagus, then sauté for 4 to 5 minutes, or until vegetables are beginning to brown.

3 Sprinkle flour over vegetables and toss well to coat. Add half of the stock, stirring to dissolve flour. Add the remaining stock and bring to a boil. Reduce the heat and simmer uncovered for 5 minutes, or until vegetables are soft. Remove from the heat and set aside.

4 Fill a stockpot with salted water and bring to a boil. Add noodles and cook for 5 to 6 minutes, or until al dente tender. Drain noodles in a colander and shake well to remove excess water. Sprinkle with olive oil (second amount) and toss to coat.

5 Reheat the ragout (if necessary thinning with additional stock). Stir in spinach and sour cream, cooking for 1 to 2 minutes, or until spinach just wilts. Add cooked pasta and mix well.

6 To serve, divide among bowls and garnish with chives.

Angel Hair Pasta with Zucchini, Herbs and Extra-Virgin Olive Oil

Serves 4

2 Tb	olive oil	30 mL
2 Tb	garlic, minced	30 mL
1	zucchini, seeded and julienned	1
	Salt and pepper to taste	
1 Tb	thyme, minced	15 mL
1 Tb	rosemary, minced	15 mL
1 Tb	chives, minced	15 mL
1 lb	dried angel hair pasta (capellini)	500 g
1 Tb	extra-virgin olive oil	15 mL
2 Tb	Parmesan cheese, grated	30 mL
	Minced thyme, rosemary and chives for garnish	
	Grated Parmesan cheese for garnish	
	Freshly ground black pepper	

1 In a nonstick skillet, heat olive oil. Add garlic and zucchini. Season well with salt and pepper. Sauté over medium-high heat for 2 to 3 minutes, or until the zucchini softens. Add thyme, rosemary and chives, tossing to mix well. Remove from the heat and set aside.

2 Bring a stockpot filled with salted water to a boil. Add pasta and cook for 5 to 6 minutes, or until al dente tender. Drain into a colander and shake well to remove excess water. Drizzle extra-virgin olive oil over the pasta and toss to coat.

3 Reheat the skillet with the zucchini mixture. Add pasta, shaking pan and stirring with tongs to mix well. Sprinkle with Parmesan and toss to coat.

4 To serve, divide among pasta bowls. Garnish with additional thyme, rosemary and chives. Sprinkle with additional Parmesan. Season with freshly ground black pepper.

The angel hair pasta cooks very quickly, so should be watched carefully. You may cook the pasta in advance. If you do, slightly undercook the pasta, drain and spread out on a tray to dry. Drizzle with a little olive oil to prevent the pasta strands from sticking together. To serve, reheat with the zucchini mixture.

Linguine with Sautéed Peppers, Orange, Garlic and Olives

Serves 4

2 Tb	olive oil	30 mL
2 Tb	garlic, minced	30 mL
1	red pepper, seeded and sliced	1
1	yellow pepper, seeded and sliced	1
1 tsp	hot sauce (or to taste)	5 mL
	Salt and pepper to taste	
1	green onion, minced	1
1 cup	orange juice	250 mL
1 lb	dried spaghetti pasta (or any pasta)	500 g
1 Tb	extra-virgin olive oil	15 mL
½ cup	pitted green olives, minced	125 mL
2 Tb	parsley, chopped	30 mL
	Freshly ground black pepper	

1 In a nonstick skillet, heat olive oil. Add garlic, and red and yellow peppers. Season with hot sauce, salt and pepper. Sauté over medium-high heat for 2 minutes. Add green onion and orange juice, then reduce the heat and simmer uncovered for 5 minutes, or until the juice has been reduced by half and peppers are tender. Remove from the heat and set aside.

2 Bring a stockpot filled with salted water to a boil. Add pasta and cook for 7 to 8 minutes, or until al dente tender. Drain into a colander and shake well to remove excess water. Drizzle extra-virgin olive oil over the pasta and toss to coat.

3 Reheat the skillet with the pepper mixture. Add pasta and olives, shaking the pan and stirring with tongs to mix well.

4 To serve, divide among pasta bowls and garnish with parsley. Season with freshly ground black pepper.

Spanish *seasonings abound in this bright and tasty dish. Olives and oranges are a natural combination, brought together in harmony by the olive oil. Use a good quality extra-virgin olive oil, and this simple dish will become a favourite.*

Wild Mushroom Cannelloni with Rosemary Cheese Sauce

Serves 4
Oven at 375°F (190°C)

WILD MUSHROOM CANNELONI

2 Tb	olive oil	30 mL
2 Tb	garlic, minced	30 mL
1 lb	wild mushrooms, sliced (chanterelle, porcini, crimini, hedgehog, etc.)	500 g
	Salt and pepper to taste	
1 cup	cream cheese	250 mL
¼ cup	Parmesan cheese, grated	50 mL
12	large dried cannelloni tubes	12

ROSEMARY CHEESE SAUCE

2 Tb	butter (or oil)	30 mL
1 Tb	rosemary, minced	15 mL
2 Tb	flour	30 mL
2 cups	milk	500 mL
½ cup	Swiss cheese, grated	125 mL
½ cup	fontina cheese, grated	125 mL
1 tsp	cayenne pepper	5 mL
	Chopped parsley for garnish	

The sauce is a variation on the classic béchamel. Other cheeses will work, but the nutty taste of Swiss (or Gruyère) cheese creates the most appealing results. Instead of cannelloni tubes, you may use fresh pasta or blanched lasagna sheets. Place a large tablespoonful (15 mL plus) of filling along one side of a 2 × 2 inch (5 × 5 cm) pasta sheet and roll up into a tight tube.

1. In a nonstick skillet, heat olive oil. Add garlic and mushrooms. Season with salt and pepper. Sauté over medium-high heat for 5 minutes, or until mushrooms are soft and appear dry. Transfer to a bowl and mix in cream cheese and Parmesan. Set aside.

2. Bring a stockpot filled with salted water to a boil. Add cannelloni and cook for 7 to 8 minutes, or until al dente tender. Drain into a colander and shake well to remove excess water. Allow to cool to handling temperature. Use a small spoon to carefully fill each cannelloni with the mushroom mixture. Place filled cannelloni in an oiled casserole dish and set aside.

3. In a saucepan, melt butter over medium-high heat. Sprinkle with rosemary and flour, stirring well to mix (do not allow to burn – reduce the heat if necessary). Add half of the milk and whisk to dissolve flour. Add the remaining milk, whisking constantly, and bring to a boil. Reduce the heat, then add Swiss and fontina cheeses, stirring until melted and smooth. Add cayenne pepper.

4. Pour sauce over the cannelloni and bake in the oven for 10 to 15 minutes, or until topping is bubbling and starting to brown.

5. To serve, use a spatula to transfer cannelloni to pasta bowls (or plates). Garnish with chopped parsley.

Sage-roasted Root Vegetable and Ricotta Lasagna

Serves 4

Oven at 375°F (190°C)

1 cup	potatoes, peeled and cubed	250 mL
1 cup	yams, peeled and cubed	250 mL
1 cup	carrots, cubed	250 mL
1 cup	onions, cubed	250 mL
2 Tb	olive oil	30 mL
2 Tb	garlic, minced	30 mL
2 Tb	sage, minced	30 mL
	Salt and pepper to taste	
3 cups	tomato sauce (p 11)	750 mL
1 pkg	dried lasagna (about 9 sheets)	1 pkg
	Olive oil as needed	
2 cups	ricotta cheese	500 mL
3 Tb	Parmesan cheese, grated	45 mL
1½ cups	mozzarella cheese, shredded	375 mL

This is a fairly traditional lasagna, but with a filling of cubed roasted vegetables. The lasagna can be made well in advance, cooled, refrigerated and reheated (some claim this even improves the flavour). To reheat, place in a 350°F (180°C) oven for about 10 minutes, or until the cheese and sauce begin to bubble. You can freeze leftovers in preportioned dinner servings.

1 In a roasting pan, combine potatoes, yams, carrots and onions. Add olive oil, garlic and sage. Season well with salt and pepper, and toss to coat. Roast in the oven for 20 minutes, stir vegetables, then roast for an additional 10 minutes, or until vegetables are soft and browned. Transfer to a saucepan and add tomato sauce. Bring to a boil, then reduce the heat and simmer uncovered for 5 minutes. Remove from the heat and set aside.

2 Bring a stockpot filled with salted water to a boil. Add lasagna and cook for 7 to 8 minutes, or until al dente tender. Drain into a colander and shake well to remove excess water. Sprinkle with a little olive oil to coat and let cool.

3 In a large casserole dish (or square baking pan), add ¼ of the tomato sauce, enough to cover the bottom of the pan. Cover the bottom of pan with 3 sheets of the pasta, overlapping slightly. Spread with ½ of the ricotta, sprinkle with ½ of the Parmesan and cover with ¼ of the tomato sauce. Add a second layer of pasta (using 3 sheets), the remaining ricotta, the remaining Parmesan and about ¼ of the tomato sauce. Add the final layer of 3 sheets of pasta and cover with the remaining tomato sauce. Top with mozzarella.

4 Bake the lasagna in the oven for 30 minutes, or until cheese is bubbling and starting to brown. Remove from oven and allow to sit for at least 5 minutes.

5 To serve, cut into portions and place on plates.

Baked Macaroni, Cauliflower, Green Onion and Brie Casserole

Serves 4
Oven at 375°F (190°C)

2 cups	dried macaroni pasta	500 mL
3 cups	cauliflower florets	750 mL
	Olive oil as needed	
2 cups	tomato sauce (p 11)	500 mL
2 Tb	basil, chopped	30 mL
2	green onions, sliced	2
2 Tb	Parmesan cheese, grated	30 mL
	Salt and pepper to taste	
10 slices	brie (about 4 oz/125 g)	10 slices

1 Bring a stockpot filled with salted water to a boil. Add macaroni and cauliflower and cook for 7 to 8 minutes, or until al dente tender. Drain into a colander and shake well to remove excess water. Sprinkle with olive oil to coat and let cool.

2 In a large casserole dish (or square baking pan), combine macaroni, cauliflower, tomato sauce, basil, green onions and Parmesan. Season well with salt and pepper. Top with brie. Bake in the oven for 20 minutes, or until cheese is bubbling and starting to brown. Remove from oven and let sit for at least 5 minutes.

3 To serve, ladle into pasta bowls.

The classic comfort food of baked macaroni is elevated to dinner party status with the addition of cauliflower, Parmesan, brie and the basil-laced tomato sauce. For a crispy coating, butter the sides of the casserole before adding the ingredients. Instead of the brie topping, substitute mozzarella, bocconcini, Swiss or white cheddar.

Rice

Cooking Rice

Makes about 4 cups (1 L)

LONG-GRAINED RICE
(BASMATI, THAI OR JASMINE)

2 cups	long-grained rice	500 mL
2¾ cups	water	675 mL
	or vegetable stock (p 7/8)	
1 tsp	salt	5 mL

SHORT-GRAINED RICE
(ARBORIO, PEARL, SWEET OR STICKY)

2 cups	short-grained rice	500 mL
3 cups	water	750 mL
	or vegetable stock (p 7/8)	
1 tsp	salt	5 mL

WILD RICE AND BROWN RICE
(WEHANI, RED OR BLACK)

2 cups	wild (or brown) rice	500 mL
4 cups	water	1 L
	or vegetable stock (p 7/8)	
1 tsp	salt	5 mL

NOTE: Before cooking wild rice, soak it in water for 5 minutes, then rinse, to remove any unpleasant flavours.

Place rice in a fine sieve and rinse well with water. Rub grains gently to remove excess starch. Drain and allow to sit for 5 minutes.

Stovetop Method:

Place rice, water and salt in a pot with a tight-fitting lid. Bring to a boil uncovered, stirring occasionally. Reduce the heat to low, cover and cook for 20 minutes. (Cook wild or brown rice for 45 minutes.) Remove from the heat and let sit, covered, for 10 minutes. Do not peek.

Microwave Method:

Place rice, water and salt in a microwave-safe casserole dish with a lid. Microwave for 5 minutes on high power. Reduce power to 50 per cent and cook for an additional 10 minutes. (Cook wild or brown rice for an additional 20 minutes.) Let sit, covered, for 10 minutes. Do not peek.

Perfectly cooked rice should be firm, with a chewy texture. Overcooked rice is mushy and starchy, and should be avoided. Once the rice has been cooked for the allotted time, remove the pot from the heat and let it sit covered (no peeking) for at least 10 minutes.

Sesame-crusted Tofu Triangles with Maple-Ginger Carrots, p 132

Fried Jasmine Rice with Broccoli and Honey-spiced Almonds

Serves 4
Oven at 350°F (180°C)

HONEY-SPICED ALMONDS

1 cup	almonds, sliced	250 mL
1 Tb	honey	15 mL
1 tsp	cayenne pepper	5 mL
	Salt and pepper to taste	

JASMINE RICE WITH BROCCOLI

2 cups	broccoli florets	500 mL
1 Tb	vegetable oil	15 mL
1 Tb	ginger, minced	15 mL
2	green onions, sliced	2
1 recipe	cooked jasmine rice (p 116)	1 recipe

This recipe is a tasty way to use up any kind of leftover rice. If you are cooking fresh rice for it, spread the cooked rice on a baking tray and allow it to cool to room temperature before proceeding. For variety, try using cauliflower, mushrooms, tofu or Asian greens. Instead of almonds, substitute walnuts, peanuts or cashews. The honey-spiced nuts may be served on their own as a cocktail appetizer.

1 Spread almonds in a thin layer on a baking tray and toast in the oven for 4 to 5 minutes, or until they just begin to brown. Drizzle with honey and sprinkle with cayenne, salt and pepper, stirring well to mix. Return to the oven for an additional 2 to 3 minutes, or until nuts caramelize. Remove from the oven and transfer to a plate. When cool, break nuts into pieces and set aside.

2 Bring a saucepan filled with salted water to a boil. Add broccoli and cook uncovered for 4 to 5 minutes, or until bright green and tender. Transfer to a sieve and rinse under cold running water. Set aside.

3 In a wok (or large nonstick skillet), heat vegetable oil. Add ginger and green onions. Sauté over medium-high heat for about 1 minute, or until fragrant. Add cooked rice and continue cooking, shaking pan gently, for 3 to 4 minutes, or until rice has dried slightly and is beginning to brown. Add broccoli, then season with salt and pepper. Stir-fry for 3 to 4 minutes to heat broccoli through and allow rice to dry completely.

4 To serve, transfer to a platter and scatter honey-spiced almonds on top.

Ginger-marinated Fruit in Coconut Phyllo Cups with Yogurt, p 146

Spice-braised Pumpkin and Leek Stew over Jasmine Rice

Serves 4

1 Tb	vegetable oil	15 mL
1 Tb	ginger, minced	15 mL
1 Tb	garlic, minced	15 mL
2 cups	pumpkin, peeled and cubed	500 mL
1 cup	leeks, sliced	250 mL
	Salt and pepper to taste	
1 Tb	honey	15 mL
4 cups	vegetable stock (p 7/8) or water	1 L
2 Tb	sweet soy sauce (p 18)	30 mL
1 tsp	hot sauce (or to taste)	5 mL
2 tsp	five-spice powder	10 mL
2 Tb	cornstarch (mixed with equal amount of water)	30 mL
1 recipe	cooked jasmine rice (p 116)	1 recipe
2 Tb	cilantro (or basil), chopped	30 mL

1 In a wok (or large saucepan), heat vegetable oil. Add ginger and garlic. Sauté over medium-high heat for about 1 minute, or until fragrant. Add pumpkin and leeks, then season with salt and pepper. Sauté for 4 to 5 minutes, or until the leeks are soft and beginning to brown. Add honey and continue cooking for another 2 to 3 minutes, or until the vegetables begin to caramelize.

2 Add stock, sweet soy sauce, hot sauce and five-spice powder. Bring to a boil, then reduce the heat and simmer uncovered for 10 minutes, or until the pumpkin is tender. Add the cornstarch mixture, stirring stir until it thickens. Check seasoning and adjust salt and pepper if necessary.

3 To serve, place hot jasmine rice in a large bowl and top with the stew. Garnish with cilantro.

The aromatic Chinese *five-spice powder usually consists of fennel seeds, cloves, star anise, cinnamon and Szechuan peppercorns. The pumpkin stew can be made well in advance and refrigerated. Reheat once the rice has been cooked.*

Japanese-style Risotto with Spring Greens, Pickled Ginger and Miso

Serves 4

1 Tb	vegetable oil	15 mL
2 cups	arborio (or sticky or sushi) rice	500 mL
2 Tb	pickled ginger, minced	30 mL
2	green onions, sliced	2
4 cups	vegetable stock (p 7/8) or water	1 L
2 Tb	miso	30 mL
1 Tb	wasabi paste	15 mL
1 tsp	sesame oil	5 mL
3 cups	mixed spring greens (spinach, dandelion greens, pea tops, mustard greens)	750 mL
2 Tb	sesame seeds	30 mL
	Pickled ginger for garnish	

1 In a heavy saucepan, combine vegetable oil and raw rice, stirring well to coat the grains. Stirring constantly with a wooden spoon, cook over medium heat for 5 minutes, or until rice turns opaque and starts to stick to the pan. Add pickled ginger, green onions and ¼ of the stock. Stir occasionally with a wooden spoon and cook for about 5 minutes, or until the mixture appears dry. Repeat with the remaining stock, adding ¼ of it at a time, stirring until it evaporates. The entire process should take about 20 minutes, or until the grains of rice are tender.

2 Stir miso, wasabi paste and sesame oil into the rice. Add additional stock if needed to make a loose mixture. Add the greens and toss well for 1 to 2 minutes, or until the greens wilt.

3 To serve, place on a platter or in a large bowl and scatter sesame seeds on top. Garnish with a clump of pickled ginger.

This *version of risotto uses Japanese seasonings and miso to bring the flavours together. For festive and tasty garnishes, look in Japanese stores for seaweed flakes (nori), toasted black sesame seeds or Japanese seasoning mixes.*

Wild Rice, Mushroom and Sui Choy Sauté

Serves 4

1 Tb	vegetable oil	15 mL
1 Tb	garlic, minced	15 mL
1	onion, diced	1
½ lb	mushrooms, sliced	250 g
	Salt and pepper to taste	
2 cups	sui choy (or cabbage), shredded	500 mL
1 recipe	cooked wild rice (p 116)	1 recipe
2	eggs whisked with 1 Tb/15 mL water (optional)	2
2 Tb	chives (or parsley)	30 mL

1 In a wok (or large nonstick skillet), heat vegetable oil. Sauté garlic over medium-high heat for about 1 minute, or until fragrant. Add onion and mushrooms, then season with salt and pepper. Sauté for 4 to 5 minutes, or until the mushrooms are soft and appear dry. Add sui choy and cooked wild rice, tossing to mix well, and stir-fry for 3 to 4 minutes, or until heated through.

2 Make a well in the centre of the rice mixture. Add egg mixture and allow to set for about 2 minutes. Chop up large pieces of egg and stir into the rice.

3 To serve, place on a platter and garnish with chives.

The chewy texture of wild rice paired with mushrooms is wonderfully earthy. This dish could be served for Sunday brunch, with a batch of potato pancakes or Potato, Corn and Rosemary Griddle Cakes (p 142) on the side.

Corn, Shiitake Mushroom and Goat's Cheese Quiche with Savoury Rice Crust

Serves 4
Oven at 350°F (180°C)

SAVOURY RICE CRUST

2 cups	cooked short-grained rice (p 116)	500 mL
¼ cup	Parmesan cheese, grated	50 mL
1	egg, beaten	1
	Salt and pepper to taste	

CORN, SHIITAKE MUSHROOM AND GOAT'S CHEESE FILLING

1 Tb	olive oil	15 mL
1 Tb	garlic, minced	15 mL
1 cup	onions, diced	250 mL
2 cups	shiitake mushrooms, stemmed and sliced	500 mL
1 Tb	rosemary, minced	15 mL
	Salt and pepper to taste	
1 cup	corn kernels	250 mL
2 cups	milk (or cream)	500 mL
1 cup	soft goat's cheese	250 mL
3	eggs	3

Rice makes a tasty substitute for pastry for this easy quiche. The dish can be made in advance and served warm or at room temperature, with a side salad. Instead of the shiitakes, try portobello or oyster mushrooms.

1 In a bowl, combine cooked rice, Parmesan and egg. Season well with salt and pepper. Pour into an oiled, springform cake pan. Spread rice evenly over the bottom and sides of the pan, using your hands to press it down well to form a dense even crust. Bake in the oven for 15 minutes, or until crust is set and browned. Remove from the oven and keep warm.

2 In a nonstick skillet, heat olive oil. Add garlic, onions, mushrooms and rosemary. Season with salt and pepper. Sauté over medium-high heat for 4 to 5 minutes, or until mushrooms are soft and appear dry. Add corn and sauté for 1 to 2 minutes to heat it through. Remove from the heat and set aside.

3 Add milk to a saucepan over medium heat and warm. Place goat's cheese in a bowl and soften with the back of a spoon or spatula. Add warm milk to the cheese and whisk to dissolve. Add eggs one at a time and mix in. Season well with salt and pepper. Fold the mushroom mixture into the egg mixture.

4 Place the cake pan holding the rice crust on a baking tray and pour in the egg mixture. Bake in the oven for 40 minutes, or until the top is golden brown and slightly puffy. Remove from the oven and place on a rack to let cool. When cool, remove the sides of the springform pan.

5 To serve, slice quiche into hearty wedges and place on plates.

Parmesan Rice Cakes Stuffed with Sun-dried Tomato, Basil and Mozzarella

Serves 4
Oven at 200°F (100°C)

AÏOLI

1 cup	low-fat (or tofu) mayonnaise	250 mL
1 Tb	garlic, minced	15 mL
1 Tb	olive oil	15 mL
	Salt and pepper to taste	

PARMESAN RICE CAKES

2 cups	cooked short-grained rice (p 116)	500 mL
1 tsp	garlic, minced	5 mL
1 Tb	minced parsley	15 mL
¼ cup	Parmesan cheese, grated	50 mL
1	egg, beaten	1
	Salt and pepper to taste	
8	sun-dried tomatoes (in olive oil)	8
8	large basil leaves	8
4 oz	mozzarella cheese, in ½"/1 cm cubes	125 g
½ cup	semolina (or cornmeal)	125 mL
1 Tb	olive oil	15 mL
	Basil for garnish	

1 In a small bowl, combine mayonnaise, garlic and olive oil. Season well with salt and pepper. Set aside in the refrigerator.

2 In another bowl, combine cooked rice, garlic, parsley, Parmesan and beaten egg. Season well with salt and pepper.

3 Wet your hands with water and place ¼ cup (50 mL) of the rice mixture in the palm of one hand. Use your thumb to form a large well in the rice. Into the well, place a sun-dried tomato slice, a basil leaf and a cube of mozzarella. Mould the rice around the filling to form a seamless ball. Flatten slightly into a patty and roll in semolina. Repeat with the remaining rice, fillings and semolina. Place the rice cakes on a plate and chill in the refrigerator for 15 minutes.

4 In a nonstick skillet, heat olive oil. Over medium-high heat, pan-fry the rice cakes one or two at a time, shaking pan occasionally, for 5 minutes, or until crisp and golden brown (reduce the heat if rice browns too quickly). Gently flip cakes over and fry the other side for about 5 minutes, or until golden brown. As the rice cakes cook, transfer them to a plate lined with a paper towel and keep warm in the oven.

5 To serve, arrange the rice cakes on a platter and garnish with sprigs of basil. Place the aïoli in a side dish.

This dish is a good way to use up leftover short-grained rice. Semolina makes a light golden crust while cornmeal makes a darker golden-yellow crust. Instead of the sun-dried tomatoes and mozzarella, try a combination of mushrooms and Swiss cheese, or roasted red pepper and goat's cheese.

Steamed Curried Vegetables and Sticky Rice Wrapped in Lotus Leaves

Serves 4

1 Tb	vegetable oil	15 mL
1 Tb	ginger, minced	15 mL
1 Tb	garlic, minced	15 mL
1	onion, diced	1
1 cup	carrots, sliced	250 mL
1 cup	cauliflower florets	250 mL
	Salt and pepper to taste	
1 cup	snow peas	250 mL
1 Tb	curry paste (p 14)	15 mL
¼ cup vegetable stock (p 7/8) or water 50 mL		
2	dried lotus leaves	2
(or cabbage leaves blanched for 5 minutes)		
1 recipe	cooked short-grained rice (p 116)	1 recipe

1 In a nonstick skillet, heat vegetable oil. Add ginger and garlic. Sauté over medium-high heat about 1 minute, or until fragrant. Add onion, carrots and cauliflower, then season with salt and pepper. Sauté for 3 to 4 minutes, or until the vegetables begin to brown, Add snow peas, curry paste and stock, stirring to dissolve curry paste. Cook until the liquid is almost evaporated, then remove from the heat. Set aside to cool.

2 Soak the lotus leaves in cold water for at least 15 minutes and drain, discarding water. Place the leaves in a large, shallow pan filled with boiling water for about 5 minutes, until pliable. Remove from the water and drain, shaking off excess water. Cut each leaf into plate-size pieces.

3 Lay one piece of lotus leaf on a flat work surface. Place ¼ of the rice in the centre of the leaf and top with ¼ of the vegetable mixture. Fold one side of the lotus leaf over the filling, then the other; fold both ends over to form a tight bundle. Repeat with the remaining leaf pieces, rice and vegetable mixture. Chill in the refrigerator until needed (can be made up to 4 hours in advance).

4 Place the lotus bundles in a steamer basket over boiling water. Cover with a lid and steam for 20 minutes. Remove the lotus bundles from the steamer and arrange on a platter.

5 To serve, use kitchen scissors to cut into the top of each lotus bundle and peel back a bit of the leaf to expose the filling.

Lotus leaves impart a distinct flavour to this rice dish, which is similar to those served as Chinese dim sum. The leaves are sold in many Chinese stores, in large bundles, and are a little fragile when dry.

Beans and Tofu

Succotash Cakes with Tomato-Basil Chutney

Serves 4
Oven at 200°F (100°C)

SUCCOTASH CAKES

2 cups	lima beans (fresh or frozen)	500 mL
1 Tb	garlic, minced	15 mL
1 cup	vegetable stock (p 7/8) or water	250 mL
1 Tb	olive oil	15 mL
1 cup	corn kernels	250 mL
½ cup	bread crumbs (or flour)	125 mL
1	egg	1
	Salt and pepper to taste	
1 cup	bread crumbs (or cornmeal)	250 mL
1 Tb	parsley	15 mL

TOMATO-BASIL CHUTNEY

2 cups	tomatoes, chopped	500 mL
	Juice and zest of 1 lemon	
1 Tb	garlic, minced	15 mL
1 Tb	ginger, minced	15 mL
2 Tb	basil, chopped	30 mL
¼ cup	rice vinegar	50 mL
2 Tb	honey	30 mL
1 tsp	cornstarch (mixed with equal amount of water)	5 mL
2 Tb	olive oil	30 mL
	Basil sprigs for garnish	

Succotash *is a traditional dish from the northeastern United States, a vegetable hash featuring lima beans. This version combines all the flavours of the original dish in breaded, pan-fried cakes.*

1　In a saucepan, combine lima beans, garlic and stock. Bring to a boil over medium-high heat, then reduce the heat and simmer uncovered for 15 minutes, or until tender. Use a slotted spoon to transfer the beans to a blender or food processor, reserving some of the cooking liquid. Add oil and pulse with just enough cooking liquid to form a thick, smooth paste.

2　Transfer lima bean mixture to a bowl and add corn, bread crumbs and egg. Season well with salt and pepper. Mix well (add more bread crumbs if the mixture appears wet).

3　In a pie plate, mix together bread crumbs (second amount) and parsley. Season with salt and pepper.

4　Take ¼ cup (50 mL) of the succotash mixture and use your hands to form into a ball, then gently flatten into a patty. Roll in bread crumb mixture to coat evenly and place on a plate. Repeat until succotash mixture is used up, should make at least 8 cakes. Chill in the refrigerator until needed (can be prepared up to 6 hours in advance).

5　In a small saucepan, combine tomatoes, lemon zest and juice, garlic, ginger, basil, rice vinegar and honey. Bring to a boil, then reduce the heat and simmer uncovered for 5 minutes, or until the tomatoes are soft. Add the cornstarch mixture, stirring until it thickens. Remove from the heat and let cool. Set aside.

6　In a nonstick pan over medium-high heat, heat olive oil. Add succotash cakes in batches and pan-fry for 4 to 5 minutes on each side, or until golden brown and crisp. Transfer to a paper towel-lined plate and keep warm in the oven until needed.

7　To serve, place two succotash cakes on each plate and top with a dollop of chutney. Garnish with a sprig of basil.

Maple, Ginger and Five-Spice Baked Beans

Serves 4 to 6
Oven at 300°F (160°C)

1 lb	white beans (navy or great northern)	500 g
2 Tb	ginger, minced	30 mL
2 Tb	Dijon (or grainy) mustard	30 mL
2 tsp	five-spice powder	10 mL
½ cup	maple syrup (or liquid honey)	125 mL
¼ cup	dark molasses (or sweet soy sauce, p 18)	50 mL
2 Tb	tomato paste (or ketchup)	30 mL
	Salt and pepper to taste	
	Vegetable stock (p 7/8), as needed	

1 Place beans in a large pot and completely cover with water. Bring to a boil over medium-high heat, then reduce the heat and simmer uncovered for 25 to 30 minutes, or until beans are tender. Add more water if necessary. Drain beans (reserving liquid) and place in a large casserole dish.

2 To the beans, add ginger, mustard, five-spice powder, maple syrup, molasses and tomato paste, stirring to mix well. Season with salt and pepper. Add just enough of the reserved cooking liquid to cover the beans. Place the lid on the pot and bake in the oven for 3 hours (add more cooking liquid if beans appear dry). Increase the heat to 375°F (180°C) and bake uncovered for an additional 30 minutes, stirring occasionally. A thick, dark sauce should coat the beans (if necessary, thin with more cooking liquid or vegetable stock).

3 Remove from the oven and allow to sit for 5 minutes before serving hot. Beans can be cooled and reheated. Will keep frozen for up to 1 month.

Baked beans are a great old-fashioned dish that has been largely pushed aside by canned versions. Soaking the beans in water removes some of the enzyme that causes gas. Vegetable-based products (like Beano®) can be purchased and taken before eating to minimize the flatulence.

Garlic and Lemon Chickpeas with Mixed Winter Greens

Serves 4

2 Tb	olive oil	30 mL
1 Tb	garlic, minced	15 mL
2 cups	canned chickpeas, drained (or dried, simmered 2 hours in water)	500 mL
	Juice and zest of 1 lemon	
1 tsp	cayenne pepper	5 mL
3 cups	winter greens, shredded (kale, mustard, beet tops, Asian greens, etc.)	750 mL
	Salt and pepper to taste	
	Extra-virgin olive oil for garnish	
	Grated Parmesan cheese for garnish (optional)	

1 In a nonstick skillet, heat olive oil. Sauté garlic over medium-high heat for about 1 minute, or until fragrant. Add cooked chickpeas, lemon juice and zest, and cayenne pepper, mixing well. Cook for 4 to 5 minutes, or until chickpeas start to brown.

2 Add the greens to the chickpea mixture and season well with salt and pepper. Continue sautéing for 2 to 3 minutes, or until the greens begin to wilt.

3 To serve, transfer to a platter. Garnish with a drizzle of extra-virgin olive oil and a sprinkling of Parmesan.

Dried chickpeas (garbanzo beans) take a very long time to cook, so I like to use canned chickpeas for convenience. Instead of winter greens, try Chinese greens such as bok choy and gai lan.

Sautéed Cannellini Beans with Mushrooms, Celery and Olive Oil

Serves 4

2 cups	fresh cannellini (or cranberry) beans (or canned, drained)	500 mL
1 cup	celery stalks, sliced	250 mL
2	bay leaves	2
1 Tb	sage, chopped	15 mL
2 Tb	olive oil	30 mL
1 Tb	garlic, minced	15 mL
½ lb	oyster mushrooms, sliced (or chanterelle, button, cauliflower fungus, etc.)	250 g
	Salt and pepper to taste	
	Extra-virgin olive oil for garnish	
1 Tb	lovage (or parsley or celery leaves), chopped	15 mL

1 Place beans, celery, bay leaves and sage in a saucepan and cover with water. Bring to a boil over medium-high heat, then reduce the heat and simmer uncovered for 15 minutes, or until beans are tender. Drain beans and discard bay leaves. Set aside.

2 In a nonstick skillet, heat olive oil. Sauté garlic over medium-high heat for about 1 minute, or until fragrant. Add mushrooms, and season well with salt and pepper. Continue sautéing for 5 minutes, or until mushrooms are soft and appear dry.

3 Add the bean mixture to the mushrooms, and season with salt and pepper. Continue cooking to warm beans through.

4 To serve, transfer to a platter and drizzle with extra-virgin olive oil. Garnish with a sprinkling of lovage.

Fresh cannellini beans are delicious when sautéed with garlic, oil and mushrooms. You may substitute fresh lima beans or soybeans. Canned cannelini beans will work, but the dish tends to be slightly overcooked and mushy. Rehydrating dried cannellini beans is a better alternative.

Oven-roasted Curried Tofu and Cauliflower

Serves 4
Oven at 350°F (180°C)

4 cups	cauliflower florets	1 L
2 blocks	firm tofu, cubed	2 blocks
1	onion, cubed	1
2 Tb	vegetable oil	30 mL
1 Tb	ginger, minced	15 mL
1 Tb	curry powder (p 15)	15 mL
	Salt and pepper to taste	
1 Tb	sesame seeds	15 mL
2	green onions, sliced	2

1 In a roasting pan, combine cauliflower, tofu, onion, vegetable oil, ginger and curry powder. Season well with salt and pepper. Roast in the oven for 20 minutes, or until the cauliflower is tender.

2 To serve, transfer to a platter. Garnish with sesame seeds and green onions.

Roasting tofu in the oven gives it a crunchy outside and a creamy inside. Cauliflower works best in this recipe, but eggplant also gives acceptable results.

Tofu Cutlets with Asian Vegetables in Black Bean Sauce

Serves 4
Oven at 200°F (100°C)

TOFU CUTLETS

2 blocks	firm tofu	2 blocks
1 tsp	sesame oil	5 mL
1 tsp	garlic, minced	5 mL
	Salt and pepper to taste	
1 cup	bread crumbs (or cornmeal)	250 mL
2 Tb	vegetable oil	30 mL

ASIAN VEGETABLES IN BLACK BEAN SAUCE

1 Tb	vegetable oil	15 mL
1 Tb	ginger, minced	15 mL
4	baby bok choys, quartered	4
1 cup	baby corn cobs (fresh, canned or frozen)	250 mL
1 cup	gai lan (Chinese broccoli) stems, chopped	250 mL
1 Tb	black bean sauce	15 mL
1 cup	vegetable stock (p 7/8)	250 mL
1 Tb	cornstarch (mixed with equal amount of water)	15 mL
2 Tb	cilantro (or basil), chopped	30 mL

1 Cut tofu horizontally into slices ½ inch (1 cm) thick, then cut each slice into 2 strips. Place tofu in a bowl and add sesame oil, garlic, salt and pepper. Toss gently to coat well. Place bread crumbs on a plate and roll tofu strips in it, coating them evenly.

2 In a nonstick skillet, heat vegetable oil. Gently pan-fry tofu cutlets over medium-high heat for 3 to 4 minutes on each side, or until golden brown. Transfer to a paper towel-lined plate and place in a warm oven.

3 In a wok (or large skillet), heat vegetable oil. Sauté ginger over medium-high heat for about 1 minute, or until fragrant. Add bok choys, baby corn cobs and gai lan. Sauté for 5 minutes, then add black bean sauce and stock. Bring to a boil and cook covered for 2 to 3 minutes, or until gai lan is tender. Add cornstarch mixture, stirring until sauce thickens.

4 To serve, arrange the tofu cutlets on a platter with the vegetables. Garnish with cilantro.

Coating tofu slices with bread crumbs results in a very crisp crust. For a thicker, richer coating, dip the tofu in a beaten egg before rolling it in the bread crumbs.

Sesame-crusted Tofu Triangles with Maple-Ginger Carrots

Serves 4

MAPLE-GINGER CARROTS

4 cups	carrots, sliced	1 L
1 Tb	ginger, minced	15 mL
1 Tb	maple syrup	15 mL
	Juice and zest of 1 lime	
2 cups	vegetable stock (p 7/8)	500 mL
1 Tb	cornstarch	15 mL
	(mixed with equal amount of water)	

SESAME-CRUSTED TOFU TRIANGLES

2 blocks	firm tofu	2 blocks
1 tsp	sesame oil	5 mL
1 tsp	ginger, minced	5 mL
	Salt and pepper to taste	
½ cup	sesame seeds	125 mL
1 Tb	vegetable oil	15 mL
2 Tb	cilantro (or parsley), chopped	30 mL

1 In a saucepan, combine carrots, ginger, maple syrup, lime juice and zest, and stock. Bring to a boil over medium-high heat, then reduce the heat and simmer uncovered for 20 minutes, or until carrots are tender. Add cornstarch mixture, stirring until it thickens. Set aside and keep warm.

2 Cut tofu horizontally into slices ½ inch (1 cm) thick, and cut each slice diagonally into two triangles. Place in a bowl and add sesame oil, ginger, salt and pepper. Toss gently to coat well. Transfer to a plate and sprinkle evenly with half of the sesame seeds. Flip tofu over and sprinkle with the remaining sesame seeds.

3 In a nonstick skillet, heat vegetable oil. Gently pan-fry tofu triangles over medium-high heat for 3 to 4 minutes on each side, or until golden brown.

4 To serve, arrange the warm carrots on a platter and top with the tofu triangles. Garnish with cilantro.

The sesame coating *adds elegance and texture to the appearance of the tofu, as well as a nutty flavour. You can substitute parsnips, yams or sweet potatoes in place of the carrots.*

Potatoes

Olive Oil and Roasted Garlic Mashed Potatoes

Serves 4

2 lbs	potatoes, peeled and cubed	1 kg
½ cup	cooking liquid (or warm milk)	125 mL
½ cup	garlic cloves from roasted garlic confit, minced (p 13)	125 mL
1 Tb	extra-virgin olive oil	15 mL
	Salt and pepper to taste	
	Chopped parsley for garnish	

1 Place potatoes in a large saucepan and cover with cold water. Bring to a boil and cook uncovered for 20 minutes, or until the potatoes are easily pierced with a fork.

2 Drain potatoes, reserving 1 cup (250 mL) of the cooking liquid. Mash the potatoes. Gently stir in ½ cup (125 mL) of the reserved cooking liquid (or warm milk). Add more liquid if necessary to make a smooth, soft purée.

3 Gently fold roasted garlic and extra-virgin olive oil into the mashed potatoes. Season well with salt and pepper.

4 To serve, place mashed potatoes in a large bowl and garnish with parsley.

This version of mashed potatoes may change your perception of the lowly spud forever. A waxy potato like Yukon Gold is best. Choose a good extra-virgin olive oil from the Mediterranean (those from Portugal are often the best value). The amount of garlic may seem excessive until you taste the rich, nutty, creamy flavour of the roasted garlic.

Mashed Potatoes with Cloves and Mustard Greens

Serves 4

2 lbs	potatoes, peeled and cubed	1 kg
3	cloves (or ½ tsp/2 mL ground)	3
½ cup	cooking liquid (or warm milk)	125 mL
1 Tb	Dijon (or any) mustard	15 mL
2 Tb	butter (or olive oil)	30 mL
2 cups	mustard greens (or spinach), shredded	500 mL
	Salt and pepper to taste	
4	mustard greens tips for garnish	4

1 Place potatoes and cloves in a large saucepan and cover with cold water. Bring to a boil and cook uncovered for 20 minutes, or until potatoes are easily pierced with a fork.

2 Drain potatoes, reserving 1 cup (250 mL) of the cooking liquid. Remove the whole cloves and discard. Mash the potatoes. Gently stir ½ cup (125 mL) of the cooking liquid (or warm milk) into the potatoes. Add more liquid as necessary to make a smooth, soft purée.

3 Stir mustard and butter into the mashed potatoes. Add mustard greens, and season well with salt and pepper. Allow the heat from the potatoes to wilt the greens (or return potatoes to the stove and stir over medium heat until the greens are soft).

4 To serve, place mashed potatoes in a large bowl. Garnish by sticking mustard green tips into the top of the mashed potatoes.

This dish was inspired by some magical mashed potatoes served to me in London, England. The soft texture of the potato can only be preserved if the cooked potato is gently mashed before adding the seasoning. Blenders and food processors are not suitable for mashing potatoes, as the result is gummy and gluelike. You may substitute arugula or Japanese salad greens (mizuna or tat soi) for the mustard greens.

Purple Potatoes Mashed with Balsamic Shallots

Serves 4

2 lbs	purple potatoes	1 kg
1 Tb	butter (or oil)	15 mL
4 oz	shallots, peeled and sliced	125 g
1 Tb	garlic, minced	15 mL
	Salt and pepper to taste	
2 Tb	balsamic vinegar	30 mL
½ cup	cooking liquid (or milk)	125 mL
1 Tb	chives, minced	15 mL

1   Place potatoes in a large saucepan and cover with cold water. Bring to a boil and cook for 15 to 20 minutes, or until potatoes are easily pierced with a fork.

2   Meanwhile, in nonstick skillet, melt butter until frothy. Add shallots and garlic, then season well with salt and pepper. Sauté over medium-high heat for 4 to 5 minutes, or until shallots begin to brown. Add balsamic vinegar and toss to coat well. Let liquid reduce to a syrup, then immediately transfer to a small bowl and keep warm.

3   Drain potatoes, reserving 1 cup (250 mL) of the cooking liquid. Let cool to handling temperature then peel, reserving 2 of the best-looking unpeeled potatoes (cut in half) for garnish.

4   In a saucepan, warm ½ cup (125 mL) of the cooking liquid (or milk) over medium heat. Remove from the heat and mash the potatoes into the warm liquid, adding more liquid if necessary to make a smooth, soft purée.

5   To serve, fold shallots into the mashed potatoes and season well with salt and pepper. Garnish with reserved purple potato halves and sprinkle with chives.

Purple potatoes are native to Peru and Ecuador, but they have recently been transported all over the globe. The small purple nugget potato is a very waxy variety that is perfect for mashing. Cook the nuggets with the skin on to retain colour and to keep the flesh from absorbing too much water. This colourful dish is perfect as part of an elegant dinner.

Baked Potato Cups Stuffed with Spinach and Morel Cream

Serves 4
Oven at 375°F (190°C)

POTATO CUPS

2	large, smooth-skinned baking potatoes	2
2 Tb	olive oil	30 mL
1 tsp	paprika	5 mL
	Salt and pepper to taste	

SPINACH AND MOREL CREAM

1 Tb	butter (or oil)	15 mL
2	shallots (or green onions), minced	2
1 Tb	garlic, minced	15 mL
4 oz	morel mushrooms, sliced (or 8 dried morels, rehydrated), or porcini, chanterelle, oyster, shiitake, etc.	125 g
	Salt and pepper to taste	
½ cup	whipping cream	125 mL
1 tsp	soy sauce (or balsamic vinegar)	5 mL
1 cup	spinach, shredded	250 mL

The crisp shells of the baked potato cups provide an attractive and delicious container for the spinach and morel cream. As an alternative, fill the cups with leftover Polish-style Chanterelle and Root Vegetable Chowder (p 53) or with mushrooms sautéed in olive oil with a little garlic.

1 Place potatoes in a large saucepan and cover with cold water. Bring to a boil, then reduce the heat and simmer uncovered for 20 minutes, or until the potatoes are easily pierced with a fork. Drain potatoes and cool with cold running water.

2 Cut each potato in half, then cut a thin slice from the bottom of each half so that it will sit flat. Scoop out the flesh (reserving it) until the sides are ½ inch (1 cm) thick. Place on a baking tray and drizzle with olive oil. Use your hands to rub the oil over each potato, inside and out. Season well with paprika, salt and pepper. Place on a baking tray and bake in the oven for about 30 minutes, or until golden and crisp. (The potato cups may be prepared in advance and gently warmed in the oven before adding the filling.)

3 In a nonstick skillet, melt butter until frothy. Add shallots, garlic and morels, then season well with salt and pepper. Sauté over medium-high heat for 4 to 5 minutes, or until the shallots begin to brown. Add cream and soy sauce, then cook for 1 to 2 minutes, or until frothy. Reduce the heat and simmer uncovered for 3 to 4 minutes, or until the cream thickens.

4 Add spinach to the morel and cream mixture, tossing to mix well. Remove from the heat and allow spinach to wilt.

5 To serve, place each warm potato cup on a plate and fill with the hot spinach and morel mixture.

Baked Chanterelles and Gnocchi

Serves 4
Oven at 375°F (190°C)

GNOCCHI

4	large baking potatoes	4
⅔ cup	flour (approximately)	150 mL
1 Tb	ground dried mushrooms (p 10)	15 mL
1 tsp	salt	5 mL

CHANTERELLE SAUCE

1 Tb	olive oil (or butter)	15 mL
1 Tb	garlic, minced	15 mL
½ lb	chanterelles (or other mushrooms), chopped	250 g
	Salt and pepper to taste	
2 cups	tomato sauce (p 11)	500 mL

GRATIN

1 cup	bread crumbs	250 mL
¼ cup	Parmesan cheese, grated	50 mL
2 Tb	olive oil (or melted butter)	30 mL
1 Tb	garlic, minced	15 mL
	Salt and pepper to taste	

Perfect gnocchi should be light and airy. Blend the dough by hand until the ingredients just come together and do not overwork. The gnocchi can be prepared in advance up to the end of step 6, cooled and held in the refrigerator for 1 to 2 hours. To serve, warm to room temperature and proceed with the rest of the recipe.

1   Prick potatoes all over with a fork and bake in the oven for 1 hour, or until soft. Remove from the oven and let cool. Cut warm potatoes in half and scoop out all the flesh into a large bowl. Discard the skins. Mash the potatoes, or push through a coarse sieve to make a soft, smooth purée.

2   Add flour, ground dried mushrooms and salt to the mashed potatoes. Use your hands to knead the mashed potatoes gently until all ingredients are mixed and holding together in a ball (add additional flour if necessary). Let rest for 5 minutes.

3   Dust the palms of your hands with flour and grab a handful of dough. Shape into a ball and place on a floured work surface. Flatten the ball and shape it into a log, rolling gently to a thickness of 1 inch (2.5 cm). Cut into pieces ½ inch (1 cm) wide. For a nice decorative effect, roll each piece over the tines of a fork dipped in flour. Repeat with the remaining dough.

4   Bring a large pot of salted water to a boil. Add gnocchi and cook for 3 to 4 minutes, or until they rise to the top. As they float to the surface, use a slotted spoon to transfer them to a plate lined with paper towels.

5   In a saucepan, heat olive oil. Sauté garlic over medium-high heat for about 1 minute, or until fragrant. Add chanterelles, season well with salt and pepper, then sauté for 5 minutes, or until all moisture evaporates. Add the tomato sauce and remove from the heat. Set aside.

6   Place the gnocchi in a casserole dish and pour on the chanterelle sauce. Toss gently to coat.

7   In a small bowl, combine bread crumbs, Parmesan, olive oil and garlic. Season with salt and pepper. Top gnocchi with the gratin mixture. Bake in the oven for 20 minutes, or until the crust is golden brown. Serve warm.

Potato, Yam and Goat's Cheese Gratin

Serves 4 to 6
Oven at 375°F (190°C)

4 cups	milk (or cream)	1 L
1 Tb	garlic, minced	15 mL
2	bay leaves	2
1 Tb	rosemary, minced	15 mL
1 Tb	sage, minced	15 mL
2 tsp	salt	10 mL
Freshly ground black pepper to taste		
½ cup	soft goat's cheese	125 mL
2 lbs	large potatoes, peeled	1 kg
2 lbs	yams, peeled	1 kg

1 In a large saucepan, combine milk, garlic, bay leaves, rosemary, sage, salt and pepper. Bring to a boil and remove from the heat immediately. Whisk in goat's cheese, then allow to sit for at least 20 minutes. Remove and discard bay leaves. Set aside.

2 Use a vegetable slicer or sharp knife to cut potatoes and yams into thin slices. Pour a ladle full of the cheese sauce into a large casserole dish, and top with a layer of potatoes. Top with more sauce and a layer of yams. Repeat with remaining potatoes, yams and sauce. Pour any remaining cheese sauce on top to cover completely (add additional milk if necessary). Bake in the oven for 45 minutes, or until top is browned and potatoes are tender. Remove from the oven and let cool for at least 15 minutes.

3 To serve, cut into squares or wedges.

Be very careful when heating milk or cream, as the liquid will expand many times in volume and overflow. Never leave a pot unattended. The flavour of this dish will benefit from cooling to room temperature and reheating in a 350°F (180°C) oven for 15 minutes just before serving.

Pan-fried Potatoes with Ancho Chili and Chimichurri

Serves 4

CHIMICHURRI

2 Tb	olive oil	30 mL
2 Tb	garlic, minced	30 mL
2 Tb	rosemary, minced	30 mL
	Juice and zest of 1 lemon	
1 tsp	red pepper flakes	5 mL
	Salt and pepper to taste	

PAN-FRIED POTATOES WITH ANCHO CHILI

1 Tb	olive oil	15 mL
2 lbs	new potatoes, peeled and diced	1 kg
1 tsp	ancho chili powder (or chili seasoning)	5 mL
	Salt and pepper to taste	
1 Tb	parsley, minced	15 mL

1 In a small bowl, combine olive oil, garlic, rosemary, lemon juice and zest, and red pepper flakes. Season well with salt and pepper.

2 In a nonstick skillet, heat olive oil. Add potatoes, and season well with ancho chili powder, salt and pepper. Sauté over medium-high heat for 5 minutes, or until potatoes are beginning to brown. Stir in chimichurri and reduce the heat to medium. Continue cooking, stirring occasionally, for about 10 minutes, or until the potatoes are well browned and soft.

3 To serve, transfer the pan-fries to a platter and sprinkle with parsley.

Chimichurri is an

Argentinian condiment that is usually served with meat, but here, mixed with ancho chili, it takes pan-fried potatoes to another dimension. Ancho chili, which is made from wood-smoked and dried chilies, is a major component of most commercial chili seasoning powders.

New Potato and Sweet Pepper Sauté with Chive Vinaigrette

Serves 4 to 6

CHIVE VINAIGRETTE

2 Tb	mustard	30 mL
1 Tb	white wine vinegar	15 mL
1 Tb	water	15 mL
¼ cup	olive oil	50 mL
2 Tb	chives, minced	30 mL
	Salt and pepper to taste	

POTATO AND SWEET PEPPER SAUTÉ

2 lbs	new baby potatoes	1 kg
1 Tb	olive oil	15 mL
1 cup	red onions, diced	250 mL
1 cup	red peppers, seeded and diced	250 mL
1 cup	yellow peppers, seeded and diced	250 mL
	Salt and pepper to taste	
	Minced chives for garnish	

1 In a bowl, mix together mustard, white wine vinegar and water. Whisk in olive oil in a slow steady stream until a smooth emulsion is formed. Add chives, then season well with salt and pepper. Mix well and set aside.

2 Place potatoes in a large saucepan and cover with water. Bring to a boil and cook uncovered for 8 to 10 minutes, or until potatoes are tender. Drain, then cool under cold running water. Cut potatoes into quarters.

3 In a nonstick skillet, heat olive oil. Add potatoes, red onions, and red and yellow peppers. Season well with salt and pepper. Sauté over medium-high heat for 10 minutes, or until potatoes are brown and vegetables are soft. Add vinaigrette and toss well to mix.

4 To serve, transfer to a platter and sprinkle with chives.

New potatoes are one of the surest signs that spring has arrived and summer is just around the corner. Choose potatoes that are firm and plump, as new potatoes can turn bad very quickly (one rotten potato can ruin a whole bag).

Potato, Corn and Rosemary Griddle Cakes

Serves 4 to 6
Oven at 200°F (100°C)

2	eggs	2
1 Tb	vegetable oil (or melted butter)	15 mL
1 Tb	rosemary, minced	15 mL
1 cup	corn kernels	250 mL
2 lbs	potatoes, peeled and grated	1 kg
2 Tb	flour (or bread crumbs)	30 mL
1 tsp	baking powder	5 mL
	Salt and pepper to taste	
2 Tb	vegetable oil (second amount)	30 mL

1 In a bowl, whisk together eggs and 1 tablespoon (15 mL) vegetable oil. Stir in rosemary, corn and grated potatoes. Sprinkle with flour and baking powder, then season well with salt and pepper. Stir well to mix.

2 In a nonstick skillet, heat vegetable oil (second amount). Drop about ¼ cup (50 mL) of batter into the skillet for each griddle cake, making 4 at a time. Pan-fry over medium-high heat for 5 minutes per side, or until golden brown (reduce the heat if the cakes brown too quickly). Transfer to a plate and keep warm in the oven. Repeat with the remaining batter.

3 To serve, arrange the griddle cakes on a platter.

A variation on the traditional latkes, these potato pancakes may be served as a side dish or as an accompaniment to a special breakfast or brunch. These cakes do not keep well if made in advance, so make them close to the serving time.

Potato, Cheddar and Green Onion Rösti

Serves 4
Oven at 200°F (100°C)

2 lbs	potatoes, peeled and grated	1 kg
1 cup	cheddar cheese, shredded	250 mL
2	green onions, sliced	2
	Salt and pepper to taste	
2 Tb	vegetable oil	30 mL

1 In a bowl, combine grated potatoes, cheese and green onions. Season well with salt and pepper.

2 In a nonstick skillet, heat vegetable oil. Drop about ¼ cup (50 mL) of the potato mixture into the skillet for each rösti, making 4 at a time. Pan-fry over medium-high heat for 5 minutes per side, or until golden brown (reduce the heat if the cakes brown too quickly). Press rösti gently to flatten and expel any excess liquid or oil. Transfer to a plate lined with paper towels and keep warm in the oven. Repeat with the remaining potato mixture.

3 To serve, arrange the rösti on a platter.

Many types of potatoes work well in this dish, but large baking potatoes are the easiest to work with. Grate the potatoes just before mixing (cover unused potatoes with a piece of plastic film to prevent them from turning an unattractive grey-brown). Drizzling the potato with a little oil helps to slow the oxidation process.

Desserts

Ginger-marinated Fruit in Coconut Phyllo Cups with Yogurt

Serves 4

Oven at 350°F (180°C)

GINGER-MARINATED FRUIT

1 cup	ginger-citrus syrup (p 16)	250 mL
1 cup	mango, peeled and diced	250 mL
1 cup	cantaloupe (or honeydew), peeled and diced	250 mL
1 cup	seedless grapes	250 mL
1 cup	strawberries	250 mL
1	apple, cored and sliced	1
1	banana, peeled and sliced	1

COCONUT PHYLLO CUPS

3 sheets	store-bought phyllo pastry	3 sheets
2 Tb	melted butter (or vegetable oil)	30 mL
¼ cup	dried shredded coconut	50 mL
2 Tb	brown sugar	30 mL

2 cups	yogurt (or soft dessert tofu)	500 mL

Sprigs of mint (or lemon balm) for garnish

The dramatic presentation of local or tropical fruit in a crisp phyllo cup elevates fruit salad to new heights. The pastry will take on the shape of whatever you mould it onto, such as tea cups, ramekins or assorted ovenproof objects to create unusual shapes. Bottled candied ginger in syrup is a good substitute for the Ginger-Citrus Syrup.

1 In a bowl, combine ginger-citrus syrup, mango, cantaloupe, grapes, strawberries, apple and banana. Mix well and let sit for at least 15 minutes.

2 On a flat work surface, lay down a phyllo sheet and brush it with melted butter. (Place the remaining sheets under a damp kitchen towel.) Sprinkle ½ of the coconut and ½ of the brown sugar evenly over it, then top with a second sheet of phyllo. Brush the second sheet with melted butter and top with the remaining coconut and brown sugar. Place the third phyllo sheet on top and brush with melted butter. Cut the layered phyllo into 4 equal squares.

3 Place an ovenproof, well-oiled ramekin upside-down on a baking sheet and gently drape a phyllo square over it. Use your hands to mould the phyllo square around the ramekin and onto the baking sheet. Repeat with the remaining phyllo squares. Place the baking sheet in the oven and bake for 5 minutes, or until the pastry is golden and crisp. Remove from oven and let cool. Remove the phyllo cups from the ramekins and set aside.

4 To serve, place a phyllo cup on each dessert plate and fill with ½ cup (125 mL) yogurt. (If the phyllo cup is tipping, put a spoonful of yogurt on the plate and set the cup in it.) Top with the marinated fruit and garnish with a sprig of mint.

Blackberries and Honey-Lavender Custard

Serves 4
Preheat broiler when needed

2 cups	whipping cream (or milk)	500 mL
1 Tb	lavender flowers (organically grown)	15 mL
4	egg yolks	4
¼ cup	liquid honey	50 mL
4 cups	blackberries (or raspberries)	1 L

1 In a large saucepan, combine whipping cream and lavender. Over high heat, bring just to a boil, watching carefully, and immediately remove from the heat.

2 In a bowl, whisk together egg yolks and honey, until yolks are pale yellow and smooth. Pour ⅓ of the hot whipping cream into the yolks, stirring well. Pour the yolk mixture into the saucepan of whipping cream. Place the saucepan over medium heat and stir continuously until the mixture thickens (it should coat the back of a spoon evenly). Do not allow the mixture to boil.

3 Strain the cream mixture into a bowl and let cool to room temperature (may be placed in a bowl of ice cubes to cool more quickly). Chill in the refrigerator for 30 minutes. (Can be made well in advance and refrigerated.)

The technique of infusing lavender in a custard was taught to me by my friend and creative chef Anthony Hodda. It may seem odd to cook with a herb associated with potpourri, but the floral note of the lavender showcases the flavour and texture of ripe berries like nothing else. This dessert can be assembled in advance and placed under a broiler just before serving.

4 To serve, divide berries among heatproof dishes and top with the cream mixture. Place the dishes on a baking tray and broil for 2 to 3 minutes, or until the topping begins to bubble and brown. Remove from the oven and serve warm.

Banana and Ginger Custard Pie with Sweet Rice Crust

Serves 6 to 8
Oven at 350°F (180°C)

SWEET RICE CRUST

1 ½ cups	cooked short-grained rice (p 116)	375 mL
½ cup	brown sugar	125 mL
2	egg whites (reserve yolks for filling)	2
1 tsp	pure vanilla extract	5 mL
	Vegetable oil as needed	

BANANA AND GINGER CUSTARD FILLING

2 cups	milk	500 mL
½ cup	sugar	125 mL
2 Tb	cornstarch	30 mL
2	egg yolks	2
1 tsp	pure vanilla extract	5 mL
1 Tb	candied ginger, minced	15 mL
1 cup	bananas, peeled and sliced	250 mL
	Strips of candied ginger for garnish	

1.   In a bowl, mix together cooked rice, brown sugar, egg whites and vanilla. Pour into an oiled 9-inch (25 cm) pie plate, spreading evenly over the bottom and sides. Use your hands to press down well to form an even crust. Refrigerate for 5 minutes. Bake in the oven for 20 minutes, or until firm and crisp.

2. In a large saucepan over high heat, bring the milk just to a boil, watching carefully, and immediately remove from the heat.

3. Meanwhile, in a bowl, whisk together sugar, cornstarch and egg yolks, or until yolks become pale yellow and smooth. Pour ⅓ of the hot milk into the yolk mixture, stirring well. Pour the yolk mixture into the saucepan of hot milk. Place the saucepan over medium heat, stirring constantly, until the mixture just boils. Immediately remove from the heat and stir to thicken and cool mixture.

4. Fold vanilla, candied ginger and bananas into the custard, mixing well. Pour the filling into the prepared crust and refrigerate until firm, at least 2 hours.

5. To serve, cut pie into slices and garnish with strips of candied ginger.

A fresh take on banana cream pie, this dessert is well worth the effort. The versatile crust can be used for a wide variety of pies. One variation is to fill the pie shell with thinly sliced apples sautéed in a little maple syrup.

Five-Spice Apples
Topped with Sesame Cobbler

Serves 6 to 8
Oven at 350°F (180°C)

SESAME COBBLER

I	egg (or 2 egg whites)	I
¼ cup	maple syrup (or liquid honey)	50 mL
I tsp	sesame oil	5 mL
¼ cup	applesauce	50 mL
I tsp	pure almond extract	5 mL
I cup	flour (or rice flour)	250 mL
2 tsp	baking soda	10 mL
pinch	salt	pinch
2 Tb	toasted (or black) sesame seeds	30 mL

FIVE-SPICE APPLES

6 cups	apples, diced	1.5 L
¼ cup	maple syrup (or liquid honey)	50 mL
2 tsp	five-spice powder	10 mL
I tsp	cornstarch	5 mL
	Vanilla ice cream (or frozen yogurt or tofu) as needed	

1 In a bowl, whip egg until frothy. Stir in maple syrup, sesame oil, applesauce and almond extract. In a sieve over the bowl, combine flour, baking soda and salt. Shake into egg mixture and fold in to incorporate. Stir in sesame seeds and set aside.

2 In a large casserole dish, combine apples, maple syrup and five-spice powder. Sprinkle with cornstarch and blend in. Pour sesame cobbler batter over top and bake in the oven for 30 minutes, or until cobbler is crispy and golden. Remove from the oven and let rest for at least 10 minutes before serving. (Can be made well ahead, refrigerated and reheated.)

3 To serve, spoon warm cobbler into serving bowls or plates and top with a scoop of ice cream.

Apples and Chinese five-spice powder are a great combination, no doubt helped by the cinnamon in the traditional mix. Try not to overwork the cobbler topping when mixing. For best results, choose a sweet cooking apple like the Fuji or Braeburn.

Strawberry and Rhubarb Compote with Coconut Crumble

Serves 6 to 8

Oven at 350°F (180°C)

COCONUT CRUMBLE

1 cup	flour (or rice flour)	250 mL
1 cup	rolled oats (or flaked or quick-cooking)	250 mL
½ cup	brown sugar	125 mL
1 cup	dried shredded coconut	250 mL
pinch	salt	pinch
½ cup	melted butter (or vegetable oil)	125 mL
¼ cup	applesauce	50 mL

STRAWBERRY AND RHUBARB COMPOTE

2 cups	rhubarb (fresh or frozen), thinly sliced	500 mL
1 cup	apple juice (or water)	250 mL
1 cup	brown sugar	250 mL
	Juice and zest of 1 lemon	
1 Tb	cornstarch (mixed with equal amount of water)	15 mL
	Butter as needed	
4 cups	strawberries, sliced	1 L
	Vanilla ice cream (or frozen yogurt or tofu) as needed	

1 In a bowl, combine flour, rolled oats, brown sugar, coconut and salt. Stir in melted butter and applesauce. Set aside.

2 In a nonreactive saucepan, combine rhubarb, apple juice, brown sugar, lemon juice and zest. Bring to a boil, then reduce the heat and simmer uncovered for 10 minutes, or until rhubarb is tender. Add cornstarch mixture and stir for about 1 minute, or until thickened. Remove from the heat and set aside.

3 In a buttered casserole, mix together rhubarb and strawberries. Top evenly with the coconut crumble. Bake in the oven for 40 minutes, or until the filling is bubbling and the crumble is golden brown. Remove from the oven and let rest for at least 10 minutes before serving. (Can be made well ahead and reheated for 10 minutes in a 350°F/180°C oven.)

4 To serve, spoon into bowls or dessert plates and top with a scoop of vanilla ice cream.

Please wait until local strawberries are in season before you attempt this dish. Imported strawberries are generally chosen for their hardiness and rapid growth rather than flavour. To extend the season, you can freeze local strawberries with good results.

◆◆

Maple-caramelized Apple and Pecan Strudel

Serves 4 to 6
Oven at 400°F (200°C)

APPLE AND PECAN STRUDEL

1 Tb	butter (or vegetable oil)	15 mL
4 cups	apples, sliced	1 L
¼ cup	maple syrup (or liquid honey)	50 mL
4 sheets	store-bought phyllo pastry	4 sheets
2 Tb	melted butter (or vegetable oil)	30 mL
3 Tb	toasted pecans, finely chopped	45 mL
2 Tb	brown sugar	30 mL
1 cup	whole pecans (or sliced hazelnuts), toasted	250 mL

MAPLE YOGURT

1 cup	firm-style natural yogurt	250 mL
1 Tb	maple syrup (or liquid honey)	15 mL

A tart cooking apple like the Granny Smith works well in this simple recipe. You can make the strudels well in advance, coating the surface well with melted butter to prevent the pastry form drying and cracking.

1   In a nonstick skillet, melt butter. Sauté apples over medium-high heat for 3 to 4 minutes, or until soft and beginning to brown. Stir in maple syrup and cook for 1 to 2 minutes, or until the syrup is absorbed and the apples are very soft. Remove from the heat and let cool to room temperature.

2   Lay one sheet of phyllo pastry on a flat work surface. (Place the remaining sheets under a damp kitchen towel.) Brush with melted butter and sprinkle with ⅓ of the chopped pecans and ⅓ of the brown sugar. Repeat the process with 2 more sheets of phyllo, melted butter and the remaining chopped pecans and brown sugar. Finish with a fourth layer of phyllo just brushed with melted butter.

3   Place the layered phyllo on a baking sheet covered with baking paper. Lay the cooled apples and whole pecans in a compact strip near the bottom edge of the phyllo. Fold the bottom edge of the phyllo over the filling, mould into a log, then roll up into a tight cylinder. Brush the top edge with a little butter and press lightly to seal. (Can be made ahead up to this point and refrigerated for 2 to 3 hours. Brush with melted butter or oil to prevent drying.)

4   Place the strudel, seam side down, on a baking sheet covered with baking paper. Bake in the oven for 15 minutes, or until crisp and golden. Pick up the sides of the baking paper and carefully transfer the strudel to a cutting board. Cut into 4 to 6 slices.

5   In a small bowl, mix together yogurt and maple syrup.

6   To serve, place a slice of strudel on each dessert plate and top with drizzle of maple yogurt.

Pear and Lychee Tarte Tatin

Serves 4 to 6
Oven at 375°F (190°C)

CREAM CHEESE PASTRY

¼ cup	cream cheese	50 mL
¼ cup	butter	50 mL
2 Tb	brown sugar	30 mL
1 ¼ cups	flour	300 mL
pinch	salt	pinch

PEAR AND LYCHEE GLAZE

1 can	lychees in syrup	1 can
1 Tb	butter (optional)	15 mL
6 cups	pears, cored and sliced	1.5 L

This foolproof, cream cheese pastry may be used for all types of baking. It makes a particularly good dough for turnovers stuffed with cooked fruit. If the pastry becomes too soft to handle, refrigerate it for 20 minutes, or until firm enough to handle, before proceeding. Choose firm pears, as they will be cooked twice (caramelized then baked).

1   In the bowl of a mixer, combine cream cheese, butter and brown sugar. With a paddle attachment, beat until smooth. Slowly mix in flour and salt. With a spatula, transfer to a small, floured bowl and cover with plastic film. Refrigerate for at least 1 hour.

2   Drain lychee nuts (reserve and set aside) and pour the syrup into a large, ovenproof skillet. Bring the syrup to a boil over high heat and reduce for about 10 minutes, or until the syrup starts to brown on the edges. Add butter (optional), stirring until the mixture turns an even caramel colour. Add pears and lychees, and continue cooking uncovered for 10 minutes, or until pears are soft and covered in a thick caramel sauce. Stir constantly to dissolve caramel lumps and evaporate pear juices. Remove from the heat and let cool slightly.

3   Place the chilled dough on a floured work surface. Use a rolling pin to roll out the chilled dough into an even circle, slightly larger than the ovenproof skillet. Fold dough circle in two, gently lift up and place over one half of skillet. Unfold the pastry to completely cover the skillet and adjust the pastry to loosely fit. Bake in the oven for 40 minutes, or until the pastry turns golden brown.

4   Remove from the oven and let cool to room temperature. Use a knife to loosen the edges of the crust, then shake the skillet gently to loosen the filling. Place a large plate over the skillet, then flip the skillet over to release the tarte onto the plate. Remove any glaze that sticks to the pan and readjust the topping if necessary.

5   To serve, cut into wedges. (Delicious with a dollop of maple yogurt, p 151.)

Honey-poached Peach and Lemon Grass Granita

Serves 4 to 6

6	large peaches, peeled, halved and pitted	6
2 cups	dry white wine	500 mL
½ cup	honey	125 mL
2 Tb	lemon grass, chopped	30 mL
	Mint sprigs for garnish	
	Peach slices for garnish	

1 In a saucepan, combine peaches, wine, honey and lemon grass. Bring to a boil over medium-high heat, then reduce the heat and simmer uncovered for 15 minutes. Remove from the heat and let cool to room temperature.

2 Use a slotted spoon to transfer the peaches (reserve 1 peach half to cut into slices for garnish) to a blender or food processor. Use a sieve to strain the cooking syrup onto the peaches. Purée the mixture.

3 Transfer the purée to a shallow casserole dish or baking pan and place in the freezer for 30 minutes. Stir to distribute ice crystals and return to the freezer. Keep stirring every 30 minutes until a smooth and fluffy mass of ice crystals forms. The entire freezing process should take about 2 hours. Cover with plastic film. (Will keep frozen for 1 to 2 days.)

4 To serve, chill martini glasses and fill with the granita mixture. Garnish with a sprig of mint and a slice of peach on the rim.

This dish serves as a refreshing way to cleanse the palate during a sophisticated multicourse meal or as an elegant finish to a summer dinner. Pears will also work very well in this dish; poach in dry white wine for about 20 minutes, or until tender. For an attractive presentation, rub the rims of the martini glasses with a slice of peach or lemon and dip into a plate of sugar.

Blueberry Johnnycake with Lemon-Sour Cream Topping

Serves 6 to 8
Oven at 400°F (200°C)

BLUEBERRY JOHNNYCAKE

1 cup	flour (or rice flour)	250 mL
1 cup	yellow cornmeal	250 mL
pinch	salt	pinch
1 Tb	baking powder	15 mL
2	eggs	2
¼ cup	liquid honey	50 mL
1 cup	buttermilk (or milk or rice milk)	250 mL
2 Tb	melted butter (or vegetable oil)	30 mL
1 cup	blueberries (fresh or frozen)	250 mL
1 Tb	flour (or rice flour)	15 mL
	Butter as needed	

LEMON-SOUR CREAM TOPPING

1 cup	sour cream (or tofu yogurt)	250 mL
2 Tb	liquid honey	30 mL
	Juice and zest of 1 lemon	

1 Into a bowl, sift 1 cup (250 mL) flour, cornmeal, salt and baking powder. Make a well in the centre and add eggs, honey, buttermilk and melted butter. Mix just until ingredients come together (do not overmix).

2 In another bowl, combine blueberries and 1 tablespoon (15 mL) flour (second amount). Toss to coat, then fold into the batter. Pour into a buttered cast-iron skillet or casserole dish and bake in the oven for 15 minutes, or until the cake rises and begins to colour.

3 Meanwhile, in a third bowl, combine sour cream, honey, lemon juice and zest. Mix well until smooth. Remove the johnnycake from the oven (leave oven on) and spread the sour cream mixture evenly over it. Return to the oven for 10 minutes.

4 Remove from the oven and place on a wire rack to cool to room temperature.

5 To serve, cut cake into wedges.

A johnnycake is a traditional New England version of sweet cornbread. For an elegant presentation, sprinkle the sour cream topping with granulated sugar and caramelize it under the broiler.

Dark Chocolate, Almond and Apricot Biscotti

Makes 4 dozen
Oven at 375°F (190°C)

BASIC BISCOTTI DOUGH

½ cup	butter	125 mL
1½ cups	brown sugar	375 mL
4	eggs	4
1 tsp	pure vanilla extract	5 mL
4 cups	flour (and a bit)	1 L
1 tsp	salt	5 mL
1 Tb	baking powder	15 mL

ADDITIONS

1 cup	dark chocolate, chopped	250 mL
1 cup	toasted almonds (or hazelnuts)	250 mL
¼ cup	apricots, chopped	50 mL

OR

1 cup	milk chocolate, chopped	250 mL
1 cup	cashews, toasted	250 mL

OR

1 cup	white chocolate, chopped	250 mL
¼ cup	sesame seeds, toasted	50 mL

This recipe forms the foundation for many types of biscotti. I like to keep the second baking time down to a bare minimum (really just to evaporate a little of the moisture and to crisp the cookie). This results in a moist, crumbly cookie that does not need to be dipped in coffee to render it edible.

1 In the bowl of a mixer, combine butter and brown sugar. With the paddle attachment, beat until creamy. Add eggs one at a time, beating smooth each time. Stir in the vanilla.

2 In another bowl, combine flour, salt and baking powder, then add to the egg mixture in two stages. Stir well, adding more flour if the mixture appears soft, as the dough should be fairly stiff (but do not overwork). Fold in your chosen additions (chocolate, nuts, fruit).

3 Place the bowl of dough in the refrigerator and chill for at least 15 minutes. On a floured work surface, scrape out the dough, sprinkle with flour and gently form into a smooth mass. Cut dough in half and shape into two smooth logs about 12 inches (30 cm) long. Dust lightly with flour and flatten each log into a long even rectangle, about 1 inch (2.5 cm) thick.

4 Gently pick up the rectangles of dough and transfer to a baking tray lined with baking paper. Flatten out the rectangles of dough so that each one evenly covers one side of the tray. Chill for at least 20 minutes in the refrigerator to rest the dough.

5 Bake in the oven for 40 minutes, or until golden brown and starting to crack. Remove from the oven (leave oven on) and place on a wire rack to cool to handling temperature. Gently transfer to a long cutting board and cut into slices ½ inch (1 cm) thick. Place the slices on baking sheets lined with baking paper. Bake in the oven for 10 minutes, or until the biscotti just start to brown. Transfer to a wire rack to cool. Repeat process with remaining slices.

6 When all the baked biscotti are cool, you may place in plastic bags and freeze. Will keep for up to 1 month.

Index

allspice honey-mustard dressing, 80

almonds, honey-spiced, 117

almonds, in biscotti, 155

angel hair pasta with zucchini, herbs and extra-virgin olive oil, 110

APPETIZERS *See also* Tapas

caramelized onion and garlic hummus with pan-fried pita, 26

hazelnut phyllo bundles stuffed with asparagus and brie, 29

lettuce wraps stuffed with roasted yam and tofu, 31

pan-fried dumplings stuffed with sui choy and mushrooms, 28

potato canapés with Cambozola cheese and roasted garlic cloves, 32

tortilla wrap stuffed with goat's cheese, tomato, arugula and sunflower seeds, 27

Vietnamese-style salad rolls with cilantro-pumpkin seed pesto, 30

apple, butter lettuce and pecan salad, 73

apple, delicata squash and wild rice chowder, 52

apple, five-spice, 149

apple, in ginger-marinated fruit, 146

apple, squash and wild rice chowder, 52

apple and pecan strudel, 151

apple cider vinegar, about, 20

apple curry and banana squash with Shanghai noodles, 108

apricot, dried, in biscotti, 155

arugula and tomato salad, 70

arugula in mixed greens, tomato and cucumber salad, 72

arugula in mushroom, leek and greens filling, 92

arugula in sautéed mixed greens, 97

Asiago, cauliflower and green onion griddle cakes, 99

Asiago, in pizza with herbs, caramelized onions, new potatoes and three cheeses, 102

Asian-spiced root vegetable chowder over thin Shanghai noodles, 62

Asian vegetables in black bean sauce, 131

ASPARAGUS

and bean sprouts with spaghettini in black bean broth, 63

and brie stuffed hazelnut phyllo bundles, 29

charred, roll, 38

in country-style sushi salad, 41

maple, mustard and balsamic vinegar-glazed, 93

and mushroom cream, 104

in spinach fettucine with spring vegetable and morel ragout, 109

and spinach soup with herbed goat's cheese quenelles, 44

avocado and cucumber roll, 39

baked beans, maple, ginger and five-spice, 127

baked chanterelles and gnocchi, 138

baked potato cups stuffed with spinach and morel cream, 137

balsamic-roasted beet salad with hazelnut sour cream dressing, 81

balsamic vinegar, about, 20

banana, in ginger-marinated fruit, 146

banana and ginger custard pie with sweet rice crust, 148

barley chowder, corn and, 51

basil, about, 22

basil sour cream, 64

BEANS AND PEAS

black, soup, 47

cannellini, sautéed with mushrooms, celery and olive oil, 129

chickpeas, garlic and lemon with mixed winter greens, 128

chickpeas, onion and garlic hummus, 26

lentils, and roasted root vegetables, 96

lima, in succotash cakes with tomato-basil chutney, 126

split yellow, soup with Moroccan spices, 48

white, maple, ginger and five-spice baked, 127

BEAN SPROUT

roast garlic broth with rice vermicelli, spinach and, 56

in salad rolls, 30

in shredded lettuce and yellow bean salad, 74

shredded sui choy and carrot salad with, 80

in Singapore-style rice noodles with shredded vegetables, 106

spaghetti in black bean broth with asparagus and, 63

bean thread noodles, in pan-fried dumplings stuffed with sui choy and mushrooms, 28

beet salad, balsamic-roasted, 81

biscotti dough, 155

black bean sauce, 95

black bean soup, 47

blackberries and honey-lavender custard, 147

blackcurrant, lemon and caper dressing, 89

blanching about, 2-3

blueberry johnnycake with lemon-sour cream topping, 154

blue cheese, in butter lettuce, pecan and apple salad, 73

BOK CHOY

in Asian vegetables in black bean sauce, 131

in grilled Asian vegetables, 95

in Indonesian-style curried vegetable soup with rice noodles, 57

in mixed Asian greens with ramen noodles in spicy soy-basil broth, 61

in udon noodles with soy-roasted tomato and corn ragout, 105

bottled sauces, about, 18-19

braising greens in minestrone soup, 58

BREAD

corn, mozzarella-basil with tomatoes and olives, 100

crumbs, in gratin, 138

crumbs, in succotash cakes, 126

flat, dough, 101

flat, topped with Thai-flavoured spinach and mushrooms, 101

pita, in pita croutons, 48

pita, pan-fried, 26

pizza with herbs, caramelized onions, new potatoes and three cheeses, 102

in sesame croutons, 68

sourdough, in tomato-arugula salad, 70

brie, baked macaroni with cauliflower, green onion and, 114

brie, hazelnut phyllo bundles stuffed with asparagus and, 29

BROCCOLI

Chinese. *See* gai lan

in hot and sour summer vegetable soup, 45

in Indonesian-style curried vegetable soup with rice noodles, 57

with jasmine rice, 117

BROTH

black bean, spaghetti in, with asparagus and bean sprouts, 63

caramelized onion, with mushroom won tons, 60

miso-garlic, 12

roast garlic, with rice vermicelli, spinach and bean sprouts, 56

spicy soy-basil, and mixed Asian greens with ramen noodles, 61

butter lettuce, pecan and apple salad with mustard dressing, 73

buttermilk, in blueberry johnnycake, 154

buttermilk, in mozzarella-basil cornbread with tomatoes and olives, 100

CABBAGE *See also* Sui choy

cabbage, green, carrot and daikon coleslaw, 86

cabbage, in wild rice, mushroom and sui choy sauté, 120

Cabernet Franc, about, 24

Cabernet Sauvignon, about, 23, 24

cake, chow mein, 104

cake, Parmesan rice, 122

cake, succotash, 126

Cambozola, potato canapés with roasted garlic cloves and, 32

canapés, potato, 32

cannellini beans, sautéed with mushrooms, celery and olive oil, 129

cannelloni, wild mushroom with rosemary cheese sauce, 112

canola oil, about, 19

cantaloupe, in ginger-marinated fruit, 146

caramelized onion and garlic hummus with pan-fried pita, 26

caramelized onion broth with mushroom won tons, 60

Caribbean-spiced black bean soup with coconut sour cream, 47

CARROT

in Asian-spiced root vegetable chowder over thin Shanghai noodles, 62

and cucumber and pickled ginger salad, 84

in French country vegetable soup with egg vermicelli, 59

and green cabbage and daikon coleslaw, 86

in honey-pickled vegetables with herbs, spices and apple cider, 83

and kaffir lime and ginger custard, 94

in lentils and roasted root vegetables, 96

in lollo rosso salad, 69

maple-ginger, 132

in Polish-style chanterelle and root vegetable chowder, 53

in roast garlic broth with rice vermicelli, spinach and bean sprouts, 56

in roasted vegetable stock, 7

in sage-roasted root vegetable and ricotta lasagna, 113

in salad rolls, 30

and shredded sui choy and bean sprout salad, 80

in Singapore-style rice noodles with shredded vegetables, 106

in split-pea soup with Moroccan spices, 48

in steamed curried vegetables and sticky rice wrapped in lotus leaves, 123

cashews, in biscotti, 155

casserole, baked macaroni, cauliflower, green onion and brie, 114

CAULIFLOWER

in baked macaroni, green onion and brie casserole, 114

in green onion and Asiago cheese griddle cakes, 99

in honey-pickled vegetables with herbs, spices and apple cider, 83

and oven-roasted curried tofu, 130

in steamed curried vegetables and sticky rice wrapped in lotus leaves, 123

in sweet and sour sauce with thick rice noodles, 107

celeriac, in French country vegetable soup with egg vermicelli, 59

CELERY

in black bean soup, 47

in fragrant vegetable stock, 8

in French country vegetable soup with egg vermicelli, 59

in fresh mushroom stock, 9

and mushrooms and olive oil with sautéed cannellini beans, 129

in Polish-style chanterelle and root vegetable chowder, 53

in roasted vegetable stock, 7

in tomato sauce, 11

chanterelle and root vegetable chowder, 53

chanterelle sauce, 138

Chardonnay, about, 23

charred asparagus roll, 38

char sui sauce, about, 18

cheddar, potato rösti with green onion and, 143

CHEESE

Asiago, cauliflower and green onion griddle cakes, 99

Asiago, in pizza with herbs, caramelized onions, new potatoes and three cheeses, 102

blue, in butter lettuce, pecan and apple salad, 73

brie, baked macaroni with cauliflower, green onion and, 114

brie, hazelnut phyllo bundles stuffed with asparagus and, 29

Cambozola, potato canapés with roasted garlic cloves and, 32

cheddar, potato rösti with green onion and, 143

cream, in potato canapés with Cambozola cheese and roasted garlic cloves, 32

cream, in wild mushroom cannelloni, 112

cream, pastry, 152

feta, cucumber and red pepper salad, 88

feta with mixed greens salad, 75

fontina, in rosemary cheese sauce, 112

goat's, corn and shiitake mushroom filling, 121

goat's, dressing, 70

goat's, herbed, quenelles, 44

goat's, potato and yam gratin, 139

goat's, tortilla wrap stuffed with tomato, arugula, sunflower seeds and, 27

mozzarella, in Parmesan rice cakes, 122

mozzarella, in sage-roasted root vegetable and ricotta lasagna, 113

mozzarella-basil cornbread with tomatoes and olives, 100

Parmesan, in angel hair pasta with zucchini, herbs and extra-virgin olive oil, 110

Parmesan, in baked macaroni, cauliflower, green onion and brie casserole, 114

Parmesan, in garlic and lemon chickpeas with mixed winter greens, 128

Parmesan, in gratin, 138

Parmesan, in pizza with herbs, caramelized onions, new potatoes and three cheeses, 102

Parmesan, in sage-roasted root vegetable and ricotta lasagna, 113

Parmesan, in savoury rice crust, 121

Parmesan, in spinach salad with sautéed mushrooms, caramelized shallots, 77

Parmesan, in wild mushroom cannelloni, 112

Parmesan rice cakes, 122

ricotta and sage-roasted root vegetable lasagna, 113

Swiss, in pizza with herbs, caramelized onions, new potatoes and three cheeses, 102

Swiss, in rosemary cheese sauce, 112

Chenin Blanc, about, 23

chickpeas, garlic and lemon with mixed winter greens, 128

chickpeas, onion and garlic hummus, 26

chili bean paste, about, 18

chili sauces, about, 18–19

chile vinegar, about, 19

chilled carrot, kaffir lime and ginger custard with green curry sauce, 94

chilled peach, honey and champagne soup, 50

chilled tomato and basil soup with sun-dried tomato salsa, 49

chimichurri, 140

Chinese barbecue sauce, about, 18

chive dumplings, 51

chive vinaigrette, 141

chives, about, 21

chocolate, almond and apricot biscotti, 155

chow mein cake topped with asparagus and mushroom cream, 104

CHOWDERS

Asian-spiced root vegetable over thin Shanghai noodles, 62

delicata squash, apple and wild rice, 52

Polish-style chanterelle and root vegetable, 53

sweet corn and barley, with chive dumplings, 51

chutney, tomato-basil, 126

cilantro, about, 21

cilantro-pumpkin seed pesto, 30

citrus dressing, 84

citrus-miso dressing, 69

cobbler, sesame, five-spice apple topped with, 149

coconut crumble, 150

COCONUT MILK

in coconut sour cream, 47

in Indonesian-style curried vegetable soup with rice noodles, 57

in spinach and mushroom topping, 101

in Thai curry dressing, 85

coconut phyllo cups, 146

coconut sour cream, 47

coleslaw, green cabbage, carrot and daikon, 86

compote, strawberry and rhubarb, 150

confit, roasted garlic, 13

cooking techniques, 2–3

CORN

baby, and red pepper cones, 40

baby, in Asian vegetables in black bean sauce, 131

baby, in honey-pickled vegetables with herbs, spices and apple cider, 83

and barley chowder, 51

in hot and sour summer vegetable, 45

in Indonesian-style curried vegetable soup with rice noodles, 57

and potato and rosemary griddle cakes, 142

ragout and soy-roasted tomato with udon noodles, 105

and shiitake mushroom and goat's cheese quiche with savoury rice crust, 121

and shiitake mushroom soup with macaroni, 65

in succotash cakes, 126

cornbread, mozzarella-basil, 100

CORNMEAL

in blueberry johnnycake, 154

in mozzarella-basil cornbread with tomatoes and olives, 100

in Parmesan rice cakes, 122

in pizza with herbs, caramelized onions, new potatoes and three cheeses, 102

in succotash cakes, 126

corn sprouts, in shredded sui choy and carrot salad, 80

country-style sushi salad, 41

cream, asparagus and mushroom, 104

cream, basil sour, 64

cream, coconut sour, 47

cream, spinach and morel, 137

cream cheese, in potato canapés with Cambozola cheese and roasted garlic cloves, 32

cream cheese, in wild mushroom cannelloni, 112

cream cheese pastry, 152

creamy lemon dressing, 74

creamy sesame dressing, 86

crispy chow mein cake with asparagus and mushroom cream, 104

croutons, pita, 48

croutons, sesame, 68

crumble, coconut, 150

crust, savoury rice, 121

crust, sweet rice, 148

CUCUMBER

and avocado roll, 39

and carrot and pickled ginger salad, 84

and mixed greens and tomato salad, 72

and red pepper and feta cheese salad with honey-lime vinaigrette, 88

in salad rolls, 30

CURRY(IED)

about, 14, 19

banana squash and apple, 108

paste, homemade, 14

powder, homemade, 15

salad dressing, Thai, 85

sauce, green, 94

soup, vegetable, Indonesian-style, 57

tofu and cauliflower, 130

vegetables and sticky rice, 123

custard, banana and ginger, 148

custard, blackberries and honey-lavender, 147

custard, carrot, kaffir lime and ginger, 94

daikon, green cabbage and carrot coleslaw, 86

dandelion greens in Japanese-style risotto, 119

dandelion greens in mixed sautéed greens, 97

dark chocolate, almond and apricot biscotti, 155

dark soy sauce, about, 17

delicata squash, apple and wild rice chowder, 52

DESSERTS

banana and ginger custard pie with sweet rice crust, 148

blackberries and honey-lavender custard, 147

blueberry johnnycake with lemon-sour cream topping, 154

dark chocolate, almond and apricot biscotti, 155

five-spice apples topped with sesame cobbler, 149

ginger-marinated fruit in coconut phyllo cups with yogurt, 146

honey-poached peach and lemon grass granita, 153

maple-caramelized apple and pecan strudel, 151

pear and lychee tarte tatin, 152

strawberry and rhubarb compote with coconut crumble, 150

Dijon-Chardonnay vinaigrette, 96

dough, basic biscotti, 155

dough, flatbread, 101

dried mushroom stock, 10

dumplings, chive, 51

dumplings, pan-fried stuffed with sui choy and mushrooms, 28

EGG

in banana and ginger custard filling, 148

in biscotti dough, 155

in blackberries and honey-lavender custard, 147

in blueberry johnnycake with lemon-sour cream topping, 154

in chive dumplings, 51

in corn, shiitake mushroom and goat's cheese filling, 121

in mozzarella-basil cornbread with tomatoes and olives, 100

in pan-fried dumplings stuffed with sui choy and mushrooms, 28

in Parmesan rice cakes, 122

in savoury rice crust, 121

in sesame cobbler, 149

in succotash cakes, 126

in sweet rice crust, 148

eggplant, Japanese, in grilled Asian vegetables, 95

eggplant, Japanese, sushi, 35

eggplant, roasted, and tomato soup, 64

endive, in beet salad, 81

endive, in mesclun, pear and red onion salad, 76

fennel, in fragrant vegetable stock, 8

feta, cucumber and red pepper salad, 88

feta with mixed greens salad, 75

fettucine, spinach, 109

fiddlehead fern, in spinach fettucine with spring vegetable and morel ragout, 109

filling, corn, shiitake mushroom and goat's cheese, 121

filling, mushroom, leek and greens, 92

five-spice apples topped with sesame cobbler, 149

flatbread dough, 101

flatbread topped with Thai-flavoured spinach and mushrooms, 101

fontina, in rosemary cheese sauce, 112

fragrant vegetable stock, 8

French country vegetable soup with egg vermicelli, 59

fresh mushroom stock, 9

fried jasmine rice with broccoli and honey-spiced almonds, 117

FRUIT

apple, butter lettuce and pecan salad, 73

apple, delicata squash and wild rice chowder, 52

apple, five-spice, 149

apple, in ginger-marinated fruit, 146

apple and pecan strudel, 151

apple curry and banana squash with Shanghai noodles, 108

apricot, in biscotti, 155

banana and ginger custard pie with sweet rice crust, 148

banana, in ginger-marinated fruit, 146

blackberry and honey-lavender custard, 147

blackcurrant, lemon and caper dressing, 89

blueberry johnnycake, 154

cantaloupe, in ginger-marinated fruit, 146

grapefruit, in ginger-citrus syrup, 16

grapes, in ginger-marinated fruit, 146

lychee and pear glaze, 152

mango, in ginger-marinated fruit, 146

mango, in Thai curry dressing, 85

papaya, in Thai curry dressing, 85

peach, honey and champagne soup, 50

peach, honey-poached, and lemon grass granita, 153

pear, grilled endive and red onions on mesclun greens with balsamic dressing, 76

pear and lychee glaze, 152

raspberry, in blackberries and honey-lavender custard, 147

rhubarb and strawberry compote, 150

strawberry, in ginger-marinated fruit, 146

strawberry and rhubarb compote, 150

GAI LAN

about, 61

in Asian vegetables in black bean sauce, 131

in grilled Asian vegetables, 95

in mixed Asian greens with ramen noodles in spicy soy-basil broth, 61

GARLIC

about, 21

confit, roasted, 13

and lemon chickpeas with mixed winter greens, 128

roasted, mashed potatoes, 134

Gewürztraminer, about, 23

ginger, about, 22

ginger-citrus syrup, 16

ginger-marinated fruit in coconut phyllo cups with yogurt, 146

ginger-sautéed spinach with miso and sunflower seed pesto, 98

glaze, maple mustard and balsamic vinegar, 93

glaze, pear and lychee, 152

glaze, teriyaki, 40

gnocchi and baked chanterelles, 138

goat's cheese, corn and shiitake mushroom filling, 121

goat's cheese, herbed, quenelles, 44

goat's cheese, potato and yam gratin, 139

goat's cheese, tortilla wrap stuffed with tomato, arugula, sunflower seeds and, 27

goat's cheese dressing, 70

granita, honey-poached peach and lemon grass, 153

grapefruit, in ginger-citrus syrup, 16

grapes, in ginger-marinated fruit, 146

gratin, 138

gratin, potato, yam and goat's cheese, 139

gravy, miso-garlic, 12

green bean and yellow bean salad with Thai curry dressing, 85

green beans and grilled peppers with mesclun salad, 71

green cabbage, carrot and daikon coleslaw with creamy sesame dressing, 86

green curry sauce, 94

green olive vinaigrette, 75

GREENS See also cabbage, Sui choy

Asian, in mixed greens, tomato and cucumber salad, 72

braising, in mushroom, leek and greens filling, 92

braising, with minestrone soup, 58

dandelion, in sautéed mixed greens with hazelnuts, 97

mustard, and cloves with mashed potatoes, 135

mustard, in sautéed mixed greens with hazelnuts, 97

spring, and pickled ginger and miso with Japanese-style risotto, 119

winter, garlic and lemon chickpeas with, 128

griddle cakes, cauliflower, green onion and Asiago cheese, 99

griddle cakes, potato, corn and rosemary, 142

grilled Asian vegetables with black bean sauce, 95

grilled endive, pear and red onions on mesclun greens with balsamic dressing, 76

grilling, about, 3

HAZELNUT

in apple and pecan strudel, 151

in biscotti, 155

pesto, 58

phyllo bundles stuffed with asparagus and brie, 29

with sautéed mixed greens, 97

sour cream dressing, 81

in tomato-arugula salad, 70

herbed goat's cheese quenelles, 44

herbs, about, 21-22

heritage tomato-arugula salad with goat's cheese dressing, 70

hoisin sauce, about, 19

homemade curry paste, 14

homemade curry powder, 15

homemade sweet soy sauce, 18

honey-lime vinaigrette, 88

honey-pickled vegetables with herbs, spices and apple cider, 83

honey pickling liquid, 83

honey-poached peach and lemon grass granita, 153

honey-spiced almonds, 117

hot and sour summer vegetable soup, 45

hummus, onion and garlic, 26

ice cream, 149

ice wine, 24

Indonesian-style curried vegetable soup with rice noodles, 57

jalapeño, in black bean soup, 47

jalapeño, in split-pea soup with Moroccan spices, 48

jalapeño, in sun-dried tomato salsa, 49

Japanese eggplant sushi, 35

Japanese-style risotto with spring greens, pickled ginger and miso, 119

johnnycake, blueberry, with lemon-sour cream topping, 154

kale, in sautéed mixed greens, 97

lasagna, root vegetable and ricotta, 113

LEEK
in fragrant vegetable stock, 8
and mushroom and greens filling, 92
and mushrooms and toasted pine nuts, wild rice salad with, 87
and spice-braised pumpkin stew over jasmine rice, 118

lemon, caper and blackcurrant dressing, 89

lemon-sour cream topping, 154

lemon-thyme vinaigrette, 97

lentils, and roasted root vegetables, 96

lettuce, yellow bean and sunflower sprout salad, 74

lettuce wraps stuffed with roasted yam and tofu, 31

lima beans, in succotash cakes with tomato-basil chutney, 126

linguine with sautéed peppers, orange, garlic and olives, 111

light soy sauce, about, 17

lollo rosso salad with zucchini and carrots in citrus-miso dressing, 69

lotus leaves, 123

lychee and pear glaze, 152

lychee and pear tarte tatin, 152

macaroni, cauliflower, green onion and brie casserole, 114

mango, in ginger-marinated fruit, 146

mango, in Thai curry dressing, 85

MAPLE
-caramelized apple and pecan strudel, 151
ginger and five-spice baked beans, 127
-ginger carrots, 132
mustard and balsamic vinegar glaze, 93
mustard and balsamic vinegar-glazed asparagus, 93
yogurt, 151

marinade, sweet soy, cilantro and sesame, 82

mashed potatoes with cloves and mustard greens, 135

mayonnaise, in aïoli, 122

mayonnaise, sushi, 37

Merlot, about, 24

mesclun greens, endive and red onion salad, 76

mesclun salad with grilled peppers and green beans in soy-honey vinaigrette, 71

MILK See also buttermilk; coconut milk
in banana and ginger custard, 148
in corn, shiitake mushroom and goat's cheese filling, 121
in mashed potatoes with cloves and mustard greens, 135
in olive oil and roasted garlic mashed potatoes, 134
in Polish-style chanterelle and root vegetable chowder, 53
in potato, yam and goat's cheese gratin, 139
in purple potatoes mashed with balsamic shallots, 136
in rosemary cheese sauce, 112
in sweet corn and barley chowder, 51

minestrone soup with braising greens and hazelnut pesto, 58

mint, about, 22

miso, about, 12, 18

miso and sunflower seed pesto, 98

miso-garlic broth, 12

miso-garlic gravy, 12

mixed Asian greens with ramen noodles in spicy soy-basil broth, 61

mixed greens, tomato and cucumber with wasabi-chive vinaigrette, 72

mixed greens with feta cheese, spiced pumpkin seeds and green olive vinaigrette, 75

morel and spinach cream, 137

morel and spring vegetable ragout with spinach fettucine, 109

mozzarella, in Parmesan rice cakes, 122

mozzarella, in sage-roasted root vegetable and ricotta lasagna, 113

mozzarella-basil cornbread with tomatoes and olives, 100

MUSHROOM
about, 9, 10
and asparagus cream, 104
chanterelle sauce, 138
chanterelle, Polish-style, and root vegetable chowder, 53
dried, stock, 10
in French country vegetable soup with egg vermicelli, 59
fresh, stock, 9
grinding for powder, 10
ground dried, in asparagus and mushroom cream, 104
and leek and greens filling, 92
with leeks and toasted pine nuts, wild rice salad with, 87
morel and spinach cream, 137
morel and spring vegetable ragout with spinach fettucine, 109

oyster, celery and olive oil with sautéed cannellini beans, 129
sautéed, with caramelized shallots in spinach salad, 77
and shallots marinated in sweet soy, cilantro and sesame, 82
shiitake, braised, sushi, 36
shiitake, corn and goat's cheese filling, 121
shiitake, in spinach and mushroom topping, 101
shiitake and sui choy, pan-fried dumplings stuffed with, 28
shiitake and sweet corn soup with macaroni, 65
in tomato sauce, 11
wild, cannelloni, 112
and wild rice and sui choy sauté, 120
won tons with caramelized onion broth, 60

mustard, about, 19

mustard dressing, 73

mustard greens in Japanese-style risotto, 119

mustard greens in sautéed mixed greens, 97

mustard greens with cloves and mashed potatoes, 135

mustard-hoisin dressing, 68

new potato and sweet pepper sauté with chive vinaigrette, 141

new potato nuggets with lemon, caper and blackcurrant dressing, 89

NOODLES AND PASTA See also soups, noodle
angel hair with zucchini, herbs and extra-virgin olive oil, 110
bean thread, in pan-fried dumplings stuffed with sui choy and mushrooms, 28
cannelloni, wild mushroom with rosemary cheese sauce, 112
chow mein cake topped with asparagus and mushroom cream, 104
fettucine, spinach, with spring vegetable and morel ragout, 109
lasagna, sage-roasted root vegetable and ricotta, 113
linguine with sautéed peppers, orange, garlic and olives, 111
macaroni, cauliflower, green onion and brie casserole, 114
rice, in salad rolls, 30
rice, Singapore-style, with shredded vegetables, 106
rice, thick, with sweet and sour cauliflower sauce, 107
Shanghai with banana squash and apple curry, 108
spaghettini in black bean broth with asparagus and bean sprouts, 63
udon with soy-roasted tomato and corn ragout, 105

NORI
in carrot, cucumber and pickled ginger salad, 84
in charred asparagus roll, 38
in cucumber and avocado roll, 39
in red pepper and baby corn cones, 40
in spinach and pickled ginger rolls, 37

NUTS
almonds, honey-spiced, 117
almonds, in biscotti, 155
cashews, in biscotti, 155
hazelnut, in apple and pecan strudel, 151
hazelnut, in biscotti, 155
hazelnut, in tomato-arugula salad, 70
hazelnut pesto, 58
hazelnut phyllo bundles stuffed with asparagus and brie, 29
hazelnut sour cream dressing, 81
hazelnut with sautéed mixed greens, 97
peanut, in green and yellow bean salad, 85
pecan, butter lettuce and apple salad, 73
pecan and apple strudel, 151
pine nuts, toasted, leeks and mushrooms with wild rice salad, 87

oils, about, 19-20

OLIVE
cucumber, red pepper and feta cheese salad, 88
green, vinaigrette, 75
and sautéed peppers, orange and garlic with linguine, 111
and tomatoes with mozzarella-basil cornbread, 100
olive oil, about, 20
olive oil and roasted garlic mashed potatoes, 134
onion, caramelized, and garlic hummus, 26
onion, caramelized, in pizza topping, 102
onion, in lentils and root vegetables, 96
onion broth, caramelized, 60
orange, red pepper, garlic and olives with linguine, 111
oregano, about, 22
orzo, in eggplant-tomato soup, 64
oven-roasted curried tofu and cauliflower, 130
oyster mushrooms, celery and olive oil with sautéed cannellini beans, 129

pan-fried dumplings stuffed with sui choy and mushrooms, 28
pan-fried pita, 26
pan-fried potatoes with ancho chili and chimichurri, 140

pan-frying, about, 2
papaya, in Thai curry dressing, 85
PARMESAN
in angel hair pasta with zucchini, herbs and extra-virgin olive oil, 110
in baked macaroni, cauliflower, green onion and brie casserole, 114
in garlic and lemon chickpeas with mixed winter greens, 128
in gratin, 138
in pizza with herbs, caramelized onions, new potatoes and three cheeses, 102
rice cakes stuffed with sun-dried tomato, basil and mozzarella, 122
in sage-roasted root vegetable and ricotta lasagna, 113
in savoury rice crust, 121
in spinach salad with sautéed mushrooms, caramelized shallots, 77
in wild mushroom cannelloni, 112
parsley, about, 22
parsnip, in Asian-spiced root vegetable chowder over thin Shanghai noodles, 62
parsnip, in lentils and roasted root vegetables, 96
paste, soy, about, 17
PASTRY See also savoury rice crust; sweet rice crust
cream cheese, 152
phyllo, about
phyllo, coconut cups, 146
phyllo, hazelnut bundles stuffed with asparagus and brie, 29
strudel, apple and pecan, 151
strudel, sesame, 92
pea, split yellow, soup with Moroccan spices, 48
pea tops, about, 98
pea tops, ginger-sautéed, 98
pea tops in Japanese-style risotto, 101
pea tops, in roast garlic broth with vermicelli and bean sprouts, 56
peach, honey and champagne soup, 50
peach, honey-poached, and lemon grass granita, 153
peanut, in green and yellow bean salad, 85
pear, grilled endive and red onions on mesclun greens with balsamic dressing, 76
pear and lychee glaze, 152
pear and lychee tarte tatin, 152
pecan, butter lettuce and apple salad, 73
pecan and apple strudel, 151
PEPPERS
jalapeño, in black bean soup, 47
jalapeño, in split-pea soup with Moroccan spices, 48

jalapeño, in sun-dried tomato salsa, 49
red, and baby corn cones, 40
red, and cucumber and feta cheese salad, 88
red, and new potato sauté, 141
red, grilled, and green beans with mesclun salad, 71
red, in country-style sushi salad, 41
red, in Indonesian-style curried vegetable soup with rice noodles, 57
red, in Singapore-style rice noodles with shredded vegetables, 106
red, sautéed, and orange, garlic and olives with linguine, 111
yellow, and new potato sauté, 141
yellow, sautéed, and orange, garlic and olives with linguine, 111
pesto, cilantro-pumpkin seed, 30
pesto, hazelnut, 58
pesto, miso and sunflower seed, 98
phyllo bundles, 29
phyllo cups, 146
pickling liquid, honey, 83
pie, banana and ginger custard, 148
pine nuts, toasted, leeks and mushrooms with wild rice salad, 87
Pinot Blanc, about, 23
Pinot Gris, 23
Pinot Noir, about, 24
pita, pan-fried, 26
pita croutons, 48
pizza with herbs, caramelized onions, new potatoes and three cheeses, 102
plum sauce, about, 19
Polish-style chanterelle and root vegetable chowder, 53
POTATO
in Asian-spiced root vegetable chowder over thin Shanghai noodles, 62
baked cups stuffed with spinach and morel cream, 137
canapés with Cambozola cheese and roasted garlic cloves, 32
and cheddar and green onion rösti, 143
and corn and rosemary griddle cakes, 142
in delicata squash, apple and wild rice chowder, 52
gnocchi and baked chanterelles, 138
mashed, purple, with balsamic shallots, 136
mashed, roasted garlic and olive oil, 134
mashed with cloves and mustard greens, 135
new with herbs, caramelized onions, new potatoes and three cheeses on pizza, 102

new, and sweet pepper sauté with chive vinaigrette, 141

new, nuggets with lemon, caper and blackcurrant dressing, 89

pan-fried with ancho chili and chimichurri, 140

in Polish-style chanterelle and root vegetable chowder, 53

roasted with root vegetables and lentils, 96

in sage-roasted root vegetable and ricotta lasagna, 113

in spinach fettucine with spring vegetable and morel ragout, 109

in sweet corn and barley chowder, 51

and yam and goat's cheese gratin, 139

pumpkin seed-cilantro pesto, 30

pumpkin seeds, spiced, 75

quenelles, herbed goat's cheese, 44

quiche, corn, shiitake mushroom and goat's cheese with savoury rice crust, 121

radicchio, in sautéed mixed greens, 97

radish, daikon, and green cabbage and carrot coleslaw, 86

ragout, soy-roasted tomato and corn with udon noodles, 105

ragout, spring vegetable and morel with spinach fettucine, 109

raisins, in wild rice salad, 87

raspberry, in blackberries and honey-lavender custard, 147

RED PEPPER

and baby corn cones, 40

in country-style sushi salad, 41

and cucumber and feta cheese salad, 88

grilled, and green beans with mesclun salad, 71

in Indonesian-style curried vegetable soup with rice noodles, 57

and new potato sauté, 141

sautéed, and orange, garlic and olives with linguine, 111

in Singapore-style rice noodles with shredded vegetables, 106

rhubarb and strawberry compote, 150

RICE See also Vegetarian Sushi

about cooking, 34, 116

arborio, in Japanese-style risotto with spring greens, pickled ginger and miso, 119

basmati, tomato, honey and lemon soup, 46

jasmine, fried, with broccoli and honey-spiced almonds, 117

jasmine, spice-braised pumpkin and leek stew over, 118

short-grain, and steamed curried vegetables wrapped in lotus leaves, 123

short-grain, in Parmesan cakes stuffed with sun-dried tomato, basil and mozzarella, 122

short-grain, in savoury crust, 121

short-grain, in sweet crust, 148

sushi, cooking, 34

sushi, country-style salad, 41

wild, delicata squash and apple chowder, 52

wild, mushroom and sui choy sauté, 120

wild, salad with leeks, mushrooms and toasted pine nuts, 87

rice noodles, in salad rolls, 30

rice noodles, Singapore-style, with shredded vegetables, 106

rice noodles, thick, with sweet and sour cauliflower sauce, 107

ricotta cheese and sage-roasted root vegetable lasagna, 113

Riesling, about, 23, 24

risotto, Japanese-style with spring greens, pickled ginger and miso, 119

roast garlic broth with rice vermicelli, spinach and bean sprouts, 56

roasted eggplant-tomato soup with orzo pasta and basil sour cream, 64

roasted garlic confit, 13

roasted garlic dressing, 77

roasted vegetable stock, 7

romaine salad with mustard-hoisin dressing and sesame croutons, 68

rosemary, about, 22

rosemary cheese sauce, 112

rösti, potato, cheddar and green onion, 143

sage, about, 22

sage-roasted root vegetable and ricotta lasagna, 113

SALAD DRESSINGS See also Vinaigrettes

allspice honey-mustard, 80

citrus, 84

citrus-miso, 69

creamy lemon, 74

creamy sesame, 86

goat's cheese, 70

hazelnut sour cream, 81

lemon, caper and blackcurrant, 89

mustard, 73

mustard-hoisin, 68

roasted garlic, 77

sweet and sour, 87

Thai curry, 85

salad rolls, 30

SALADS, GREEN See also Salads, Vegetable

butter lettuce, pecan and apple, 73

grilled endive, pear and red onions on mesclun greens, 76

heritage tomato-arugula, 70

lollo rosso with zucchini and carrots, 69

mesclun with grilled peppers and green beans, 71

mixed greens with feta cheese, 75

mixed greens, tomato and cucumber, 72

romaine salad, 68

shredded lettuce, yellow bean and sunflower sprout, 74

spinach salad with sautéed mushrooms and caramelized shallots, 77

SALADS, VEGETABLE See also Salads, Green

balsamic-roasted beet, 81

country-style sushi, 41

cucumber, red pepper and feta cheese, 88

green and yellow bean salad, 85

green cabbage, carrot and daikon coleslaw, 86

honey-pickled vegetables, 83

mushrooms and shallots, 82

new potato nuggets, 89

shredded carrot, cucumber and pickled ginger, 84

shredded sui choy, carrot and bean sprout, 80

sweet and sour wild rice with leeks, mushrooms and toasted pine nuts, 87

salsa, sun-dried tomato, 49

SAUCES

black bean, 95

chanterelle, 138

green curry, 94

homemade sweet soy, 18

rosemary cheese, 112

soy, about, 17-18

soy-vinegar dipping, 28

tomato, 11

sautéed cannellini beans with mushrooms, celery and olive oil, 129

sautéed mixed greens with hazelnuts and lemon-thyme vinaigrette, 97

sautéing, about, 2

Sauvignon Blanc, 24

savoury rice crust, 121

SEEDS

pumpkin and cilantro pesto, 30

pumpkin, spiced, 75

sesame cobbler, 149

sesame croutons, 68

sesame-crusted tofu triangles, 132

sesame strudel, 92

sesame, in biscotti, 155

sesame, in country-style sushi salad, 41

sesame, in green cabbage, carrot and daikon coleslaw, 86

sesame, in Japanese-style risotto with spring greens, pickled ginger and miso, 119 sesame, in maple, mustard and balsamic vinegar-glazed asparagus, 93

sesame, in mushrooms and shallots marinated in sweet soy, cilantro and sesame, 82

sesame, in oven-roasted curried tofu and cauliflower, 130

sesame, spinach and mushroom topping, 101

sunflower pesto and miso with ginger-sautéed spinach, 98

sunflower, goat's cheese, tomato and arugula stuffed tortilla wrap, 27

sunflower, in creamy lemon dressing, 74

semolina, in Parmesan rice cakes, 122

SESAME

in biscotti, 155

cobbler, 149

in country-style sushi salad, 41

croutons, 68

-crusted tofu triangles with maple-ginger carrots, 132

in green cabbage, carrot and daikon coleslaw, 86

in Japanese-style risotto with spring greens, pickled ginger and miso, 119

in maple, mustard and balsamic vinegar-glazed asparagus, 93

in mushrooms and shallots marinated in sweet soy, cilantro and sesame, 82

in oven-roasted curried tofu and cauliflower, 130

spinach and mushroom topping, 101

strudel stuffed with mushrooms, leeks and greens, 92

sesame oil, about, 20

shallots, balsamic, 136

shallots, caramelized, in spinach salad, 77

shallots, marinated, 82

Shanghai noodles with banana squash and apple curry, 108

SHIITAKE

and sui choy, pan-fried dumplings stuffed with, 28

and sweet corn soup with macaroni, 65

braised, sushi, 36

corn and goat's cheese filling, 121

in spinach and mushroom topping, 101

Shiraz, about, 24

shredded carrot, cucumber and pickled ginger salad with citrus dressing, 84

shredded lettuce, yellow bean and sunflower sprout salad with creamy lemon dressing, 74

shredded sui choy, carrot and bean sprout salad with allspice honey-mustard dressing, 80

Singapore-style rice noodles with shredded vegetables, 106

snow peas, in country-style sushi salad, 41

snow peas, in hot and sour summer vegetable soup, 45

snow peas, in steamed curried vegetables and sticky rice wrapped in lotus leaves, 123

SOUPS See also Broths; Chowders; Soups, Noodle

asparagus and spinach, 44

Caribbean-spiced black bean, 47

chilled peach, honey and champagne, 50

chilled tomato and basil, 49

hot and sour summer vegetable, 45

split-pea with Moroccan spices, 48

tomato, honey, lemon and basmati rice, 46

SOUPS, NOODLE See also Broths, Chowders, Soups

French country vegetable with egg vermicelli, 59

Indonesian-style curried vegetable with rice noodles, 57

minestrone soup with braising greens and hazelnut pesto, 58

roasted eggplant-tomato with orzo pasta, 64

sweet corn and shiitake mushroom with macaroni, 65

sour cream, basil, 64

sour cream, coconut, 47

sour cream, hazelnut, 81

sour cream-lemon topping, 154

soy-honey vinaigrette, 71

soy paste, 17

soy sauces, about, 17-18

soy-vinegar dipping sauce, 28

spaghettini in black bean broth with asparagus and bean sprouts, 63

spice-braised pumpkin and leek stew over jasmine rice, 118

spiced pumpkin seeds, 75

SPINACH

and asparagus soup, 44

in cilantro-pumpkin seed pesto, 30

fettucine with spring vegetable and morel ragout, 109

ginger-sautéed, 98

in green curry sauce, 94

in Japanese-style risotto, 119

in mashed potatoes with cloves and mustard greens, 135

and morel cream, 137

and mushroom topping, 101

and pickled ginger rolls, 37

and rice vermicelli and bean sprouts with roast garlic broth, 56

salad with sautéed mushrooms, caramelized shallots, 77

in sautéed mixed greens with hazelnuts, 97

split-pea soup with Moroccan spices and pita croutons, 48

SPROUTS

bean, and asparagus with spaghettini in black bean broth, 63

bean, and rice vermicelli and spinach with roast garlic broth, 56

bean, and shredded sui choy and carrot salad, 80

bean, in salad rolls, 30

bean, in shredded lettuce and yellow bean salad, 74

bean, in Singapore-style rice noodles with shredded vegetables, 106

corn, in shredded sui choy and carrot salad, 80

sunflower, and shredded lettuce and yellow bean salad, 74

sunflower, in shredded sui choy and carrot salad, 80

squash, acorn, in Shanghai noodles with banana squash and apple curry, 108

squash, banana, and apple curry with Shanghai noodles, 108

squash, delicata, and apple and wild rice chowder, 52

steamed curried vegetables and sticky rice wrapped in lotus leaves, 123

steaming, about 3

stew, spice-braised pumpkin and leek, 118

stir-frying, about, 2

STOCKS See also Broths

about, 6

dried mushroom, 10

fragrant vegetable, 8

fresh mushroom, 9

roasted vegetable, 7

strawberry, in ginger-marinated fruit, 146

strawberry and rhubarb compote with coconut crumble, 150

strudel, maple-caramelized apple and pecan, 151

strudel, sesame stuffed with mushrooms, leeks and greens, 92

succotash cakes with tomato-basil chutney, 126

SUI CHOY See also Cabbage

in mixed Asian greens with ramen noodles in spicy soy-basil broth, 61

and mushroom stuffing for pan-fried dumplings, 28

in Shanghai noodles with banana squash and apple curry, 108

shredded, and carrot and bean sprout salad, 80

and wild rice and mushroom sauté, 120

sun-dried tomato salsa, 49

sunflower seed, goat's cheese, tomato and arugula stuffed tortilla wrap, 27

sunflower seed pesto and miso with ginger-sautéed spinach, 98

sunflower seeds, in creamy lemon dressing, 74

sunflower sprouts, shredded lettuce and yellow bean salad with, 74

sunflower sprouts, in shredded sui choy and carrot salad, 80

sushi. *See* Vegetarian Sushi

sweet and sour dressing, 87

sweet and sour wild rice salad with leeks, mushrooms and toasted pine nuts, 87

sweet chili sauce, about, 18

sweet corn and barley chowder with chive dumplings, 51

sweet corn and shiitake mushroom soup with macaroni, 65

sweet rice crust, 148

sweet soy, cilantro and sesame marinade, 82

sweet soy sauce, about, 18

Swiss cheese, in pizza with herbs, caramelized onions, new potatoes and three cheeses, 102

Swiss cheese, in rosemary cheese sauce, 112

syrup, ginger-citrus, 16

tamari sauce, about, 17

TAPAS *See also* Appetizers

cauliflower, green onion and Asiago cheese griddle cakes, 99

chilled carrot, kaffir lime and ginger custard with green curry sauce, 94

ginger-sautéed spinach with miso and sunflower seed pesto, 98

grilled Asian vegetables with black bean sauce, 95

maple, mustard and balsamic vinegar-glazed asparagus, 93

sautéed mixed greens with hazelnuts and lemon-thyme vinaigrette, 97

sesame strudel stuffed with mushrooms, leeks and greens, 92

warm lentils and roasted root vegetables with Dijon-Chardonnay vinaigrette, 96

tarte tatin, pear and lychee, 152

teriyaki glaze, 40

teriyaki red pepper and baby corn cones, 40

Thai curry dressing, 85

thick rice noodles with sweet and sour cauliflower sauce, 107

thyme, about, 22

TOFU

in creamy sesame dressing, 86

cutlets with Asian vegetables in black bean sauce, 131

oven-roasted, curried, and cauliflower, 130

and roasted yam stuffed lettuce wraps, 31

sesame-crusted triangles with maple-ginger carrots, 132

TOMATO

and basil chutney, 126

and basil soup, 49

cherry, and olives with mozzarella-basil cornbread, 100

heritage, and arugula salad, 70

and honey, lemon and basmati rice soup, 46

in hot and sour summer vegetable soup, 45

and mixed greens and cucumber salad, 72

and roasted eggplant soup, 64

Roma, soy-roasted, and corn ragout with udon noodles, 105

sauce, 11

stewed, in tomato sauce, 11

sun-dried, in Parmesan rice cakes, 122

sun-dried, in salsa, 49

in sun-dried tomato salsa, 49

in thick rice noodles with sweet and sour cauliflower sauce, 107

topping, lemon-sour cream, 154

topping, spinach and mushroom, 101

tortilla wrap stuffed with goat's cheese, tomato, arugula and sunflower seeds, 27

udon noodles with soy-roasted tomato and corn ragout, 105

vegetable oils, about, 19-20

vegetable stock, fragrant, 8

vegetable stock, roasted, 7

VEGETARIAN SUSHI

braised shiitake mushroom, 36

charred asparagus roll, 38

country-style sushi salad, 41

cucumber and avocado roll, 39

Japanese eggplant, 35

spinach and pickled ginger rolls, 37

sushi rice, cooking, 34

teriyaki red pepper and baby corn cones, 40

Vietnamese-style salad rolls with cilantro-pumpkin seed pesto, 30

VINAIGRETTES *See also* Salad Dressings

chive, 141

Dijon-Chardonnay, 96

green olive, 75

honey-lime, 88

lemon-thyme, 97

soy-honey, 71

wasabi-chive, 72

vinegars, about, 20

warm lentils and roasted root vegetables with Dijon-Chardonnay vinaigrette, 96

wasabi, about, 19

wasabi-chive vinaigrette, 72

white vinegar, about, 20

wild mushroom cannelloni with rosemary cheese sauce, 112

wild rice, delicata squash and apple chowder, 52

wild rice, mushroom and sui choy sauté, 120

wild rice salad with leeks, mushrooms and toasted pine nuts, 87

wines, about, 24-25

won tons, mushroom, 60

wrap, lettuce stuffed with roasted yam and tofu, 31

wrap, tortilla stuffed with goat's cheese, tomato, arugula and sunflower seeds, 27

YAM

in Asian-spiced root vegetable chowder over thin Shanghai noodles, 62

in black bean soup, 47

and potato and goat's cheese gratin, 139

roasted, and tofu stuffed lettuce wraps, 31

in sage-roasted root vegetable and ricotta lasagna, 113

yellow and green bean salad, 85

yellow beans, shredded lettuce and sunflower sprout salad, 74

yellow pepper, and new potato sauté, 141

yellow peppers, sautéed, and orange, garlic and olives with linguine, 111

yogurt, with coconut phyllo cups, 146

yogurt, in lemon-sour cream topping, 154

yogurt, maple, 151

Zinfandel, about, 24

ZUCCHINI

in chilled tomato and basil soup, 49

in country-style sushi salad, 41

in grilled Asian vegetables, 95

and herbs and extra-virgin olive oil with angel hair pasta, 110

in honey-pickled vegetables with herbs, spices and apple cider, 83

in hot and sour summer vegetable soup, 45

in lollo rosso salad, 69

in salad rolls, 30

in tomato sauce, 11